IN ANOTHER COUNTRY

Margaret Roosevelt

MINERVA PUBLISHING CO.

ISBN 1 930493 06 1

First Published 2000 by
Minerva Publishing Co.
1001 Brickell Bay Drive, Suite 2310
Miami, Florida 33131

Printed for Minerva Publishing Co.

IN ANOTHER COUNTRY

2nd Fryar: "Thou hast committed…"
Barabas: "Fornication? But that was in another country. And besides, the Wench is dead."

Christopher Marlowe
The Jew of Malta

Prologue

I think I married Sandro for two reasons. To get away from family and because I had fallen in love with Italy. I had visited the country as a tourist when I was fifteen and after that had spent two winters in school in Rome learning the language, studying art and meeting the man who was to become my husband. My parents took a dim view of the whole thing, but for the first time in my life I asserted myself, argued my case, whined and sulked until they gave in. We had a big wedding in St. James' Church in New York and honeymooned in my father's house in Bermuda, most of which time I spent in hospital in Hamilton with acute appendicitis! Then it was back to Rome to stay with Sandro's parents until our own little apartment on the outskirts of the Parioli district could be made ready. In those days it seemed very far away from everything, as the city hadn't yet spread to reach the newer residential sections. Our building stood alongside a small park with ilex trees and umbrella pines, and in the summer the nightingales would call to each other as soon as the sun went down and a damp mist came curling up from the Tiber. I think that first year was the happiest of my life. My husband and I were never separated and there was little room in my life for other people or outside things. Sometimes in the evenings we would walk down to watch the river, and on the way home we would stop at the foot of the Trinita dei Monti and he would buy me flowers, a different one for each season of the year, but the one I loved the most was the deep pink spray of flowering peach, the first sure sign of spring. On Sundays we would drive out into the country, to the lakes or up to the Castelli to sample the new wine, and on weekdays I would take a book or a pile of American newspapers and sit in the car outside his office, where he could see me from a window and know that I was close. It was a lovely life and if there was very little privacy or personal freedom I didn't at first notice. I knew that Sandro had a jealous disposition but I was confident that when he saw that there was no reason for this he would forget about it. So I tried in every way to please him, to submit to his will and to avoid doing anything that would mark me as different from the other Italian wives.

A real sense that all was not going well with my marriage didn't come until about the middle of the second year. After the novelty of our physical proximity had worn off I found we really didn't have much to say to each other. I had always been fond of reading, but Sandro took it as a personal insult if I picked up a book after dinner. He would fiddle around restlessly and try to rush me off to bed, or suggest having friends over for bridge or poker. He was a great gambler. At first I fought against these social evenings. It seemed to me that they could very easily become a habit and I felt that married life was worth little if it had to be spent exclusively in bed. For another thing my part in these gatherings was as limited as if I were confined to a harem. I was not allowed to associate with the men. It made no difference that they were friends that he had known for years. The minute he saw me in conversation he would rush up and separate us and demand from me a complete résumé of the conversation; and as for dancing, that was out entirely. The

American custom of dancing cheek to cheek had become popular, but for me it was strictly forbidden and I finally got so nervously upset by the constant interrogations – "What did he say that made you laugh like that?" "He was holding you too tightly!" – that I finally gave up dancing altogether. The last straw came when he rushed up and struck me in the face one night in the middle of the dance floor of the Quirinale garden while I was dancing with the husband of my best friend! I had always been an introspective type and this mistrust only served to turn me all the more inwardly toward myself. I grew sullen and apprehensive, with a constant feeling of guilt about I knew not what. And the more I despaired and raged inwardly, the more submissive I tried to appear. Sandro felt that nothing was wrong. I was outwardly docile and dominated and that was apparently the kind of wife he wanted. If at times I tried to explain that I felt a lack of companionship and that in America it was considered possible for a man and a woman to carry on a conversation without ending up in bed, he would reply that in Italy things were different and that would be the end of it. So I fought against my natural instincts, tried to believe that he was right and refused to admit that there were any flaws in my marriage.

At times it was hard to keep up the pretence and I grew heartily sick of the vapid, useless life I was forced to lead. My mornings were occupied at home, but the novelty of housekeeping soon wore off. We had one maid and for a while I amused myself trying to teach her to cook American dishes, but that didn't last very long because Sandro refused to eat anything new. The long afternoons sitting in the car in front of his office almost drove me out of my mind with boredom so I finally persuaded him to let me go on little shopping excursions with his mother. I was fond of my mother-in-law but these outings finally wore out my patience completely. We would drag up and down the streets peering into each window, looking at the same displays over and over again. Very little was ever bought, but old Mrs. Palmieri thoroughly enjoyed bargaining as I stood first on one foot and then on the other for what seemed like hours while she tried to knock a few lire off the price of each object. For over a year I alternated the shopping expeditions with sitting in the car and by that time we had accumulated a small circle of married friends of our own age, four couples in all, and I began to be invited to afternoon bridge teas. It was all very routine but it was a welcome change. We met first in one house and then in another, always the same five of us playing the same poor bridge and eating the same fancy little cakes from the same bakery. Sandro would phone about the middle of the afternoon to check if I was really where I said I would be and then he and the other husbands would arrive at seven to collect their wives. It was appallingly dull, but at least it disposed of two afternoons a week. I kept telling myself that this was married life and no one else seemed to chafe under its restrictions. If sometimes I longed for some masculine companionship or a conversation that didn't center on clothes, servants or children, I tried not to let on. And so another year passed before these afternoon sessions were brought to an abrupt end. I was on my way to Clara's home. It was an afternoon in early April and the warm air sweeping up from Ostia smelled of spring. The Judas trees had begun to flower in purple and magenta fantasy and the receding waters of the Tiber had left the gardens of the rowing clubs along the riverbank lush and verdant. There was a sense of expectancy, of reawakening in the brighter colors, the sharper sounds. By the time I arrived at Clara's, I was in the grip of spring fever.

"Let's all go and have tea in the Borghese gardens," I suggested. "We can always play bridge and it is much too beautiful for us to stay here." To my surprise they all consented and we sat under the wisteria vines and ate ices until the twilight chill sent me dashing to the phone to call Sandro. He was furious, "Go right home," he ordered. I felt as if I had been slapped in the face again. All the life and joy faded away as I took my leave and hurried guiltily away. At home there was another big scene. Apparently, I couldn't be trusted to do what was expected of me, I had to show myself off in public places without my husband. From now on I could stay at home. There was nothing I could do but submit. Then came the night of Sandro's birthday party. I had arranged a surprise. He and I had gone out for dinner and I faked a headache in order to get home early where a group of our friends were to hide in the bedroom. I took off my wraps and started toward the bedroom when I saw that Sandro had paused beside the telephone stand that stood in the corridor. He was looking intently at the ashtray. "Where did this come from?" he asked.

"What?" I said. "This cigarette stub. It's from an Italian cigarette. I can see the brand. You and I don't smoke anything but American cigarettes."

"Sandro, I don't know…" I began lamely. He launched into a maniacal tirade. Who had I been entertaining? What was going on behind his back? What kind of a wife did I think I was? For a moment I thought he was going to do me bodily harm, but all I could think of was our guests behind the door of the bedroom witnessing this scene. My heart leapt and fluttered and I felt cold all over. I wanted to run or to die. Fortunately, it didn't last very long. The bedroom door opened and everyone trooped gaily out pretending that nothing had happened and Sandro was caught up in the wave of festivities. He didn't think it necessary to apologize, or perhaps he forgot, but I am sure, in his arrogance, he felt he was justified. As for me, I was too hurt and upset to bother too much about my guests and although I tried to put on a good show I was delighted when the evening was finally over and I could crawl into bed to brood over the incident. Sandro never mentioned it and I had learned the futility of trying to talk things out... I felt cold and lonely and when I finally fell asleep I was shaking as if with a chill.

That night I made up my mind. From now on I would live my own life and take whatever happiness I could find. He accused me of having lovers? I would have them. He said he would kill me if I were unfaithful? Well, maybe he wouldn't find out. I hated him for what he was doing to me and for what he was making me do to myself.

Contents

Preface

Like most isms and ocracies, Fascism in practice bears very little resemblance to its textbook definitions. It is not going to be my purpose to go into the ideology, the protocol of the corporate state, nor any of the theories upon which the Fascist doctrine hinges. Having lived for over fifteen years in Italy – 1931–1945 – probably the purest example of complete degeneration of any political ideal – I was concerned particularly with the personal angle and about as ignorant of the background technicalities as would be the average American in the same circumstances. In setting down some of the following incidents, I realize that many similar conditions could arise in almost any country. However, I am an American and I cannot help but look at things through American eyes and with an American point of view. I could not reconcile myself to the Italian apathy towards existing conditions. Each new departure seemed to me more dangerous and horrifying than the last and this crescendo for me typifies the totalitarian state. The gradual encroachment of the State in the person of even the smallest of its hirelings upon one's personal life is an unpleasant experience, but Fascism cannot afford to take any chances and whoever cannot identify with it must be destroyed. The country itself was the first to lose its personality. Since 1931, when I first landed there, I did not see the word "Italy" printed by itself or spoken alone; the term was always "Italia-Fascista". If I remember rightly, it was just after the League of Nations imposed sanctions because of Italy's war in Ethiopia that the big drive for Italian autonomy really got under way. You have no idea how monotonous a word can become until you have seen it glaring at you from billboards, screaming at you from the radio, shoved down your throat in the cinema. It was always AUTARCHIA *ad nauseam* and *ad ridiculum*. To my mind the epitome was reached when parts of the language were changed by law. Every language has foreign words that have been incorporated into the vernacular; one of these was "sandwich" which, being a dastardly English word, behooved the powers that be to Italianize it, the cacophonous result of which was the word "tramezzino". (Sixty years later it is still in use, probably the only changed word that has outlived that era.) The Italian Academy then met with a list of foreign words and, after many debates, gave each one the same treatment. "Bidet" became "cavalchino", the implications of which are obvious! "Cachet" became "cialdino", "zuppa inglese" a poisonous dessert composed of sponge cake soaked in cherry brandy and covered with whipped cream, became "zuppa adua" during the Ethiopian campaign and then "zuppa italiana". "Insalata russa" underwent a similar metamorphosis. Street names were also changed; I lived on via Panama and awoke one morning to discover I was now living on viale Giappone! Even more ridiculous was the campaign to abolish the verbal third-person singular, the formal mode of address. The excuse for this was that the *Lei* was of Spanish origin and as such un-Italian. Placards were introduced in all public places with the admonition "Parlate con Voi". If you refused to *parlare con voi* you were likely not to receive an answer from the person addressed – or to end up in jail. This was all right from Naples south as the *voi* was the usual form of address, but in the north of Italy it was bitterly resented, not only for the difficulty which any enforced change of language would evoke but also because the northern Italians are inclined to look down on their southern compatriots. To be forced to adopt their manner of speaking was highly insulting. The next thing to go was the handshake (an effete Anglo-Saxon custom) for which the "Roman" salute was substituted. While this was still quite new I remember going to a reception given by Ciano for Serrano Suner just after the victorious Spanish war. I was accompanied by some friends who took these Fascist regulations about as seriously as I did. As we approached Count Ciano, Alberto automatically held out his hand. There was an embarrassing pause as Ciano gave the Fascist salute and Alberto's hand dangled in mid air. Then Ciano rallied gamely and taking the extended hand said, "Perhaps we can make an exception and shake hands on this occasion." Such a poor example of Fascist discipline in front of the Spanish guests must have been highly unnerving!

I remember the amusements I got from an item in the Roman newspaper headed "Patriotic Gesture of Three Aviators" and datelined Venice. It told of a group of young girls who were sitting on the beach playing a gramophone. As was usual in Europe, most of the records were American. Apparently, this did not meet with the approval of the young fliers who were occupying a nearby cabana because they descended on the hapless group, seized the offending American records and hurled them into the sea!

Like a gradual paralysis the encroachment crept on. With the entry into war in 1939, restriction followed restriction. To give an idea of the crescendo I will take one item and follow it; at first all orchestras, dancing and evening dress were prohibited in public; then dining out in groups of more than four people was not allowed; next, they forbade dancing to the gramophone in the home; then playing any gambling game at home; next any gathering of friends in a private house. Ignoring this, my husband and I continued to entertain until one evening, having exceeded the limit of people allowed, my husband attempted to eject the latest arrival. A fight ensued and my husband was challenged to a duel! Unfortunately – or fortunately – at the time he was suffering from two broken collarbones, the result of a fall from a horse while playing polo, so the whole affair was settled amicably by the "seconds"!

Chapter I

One evening, we were sitting in the living room of Mario Camerini, an Italian film director who had distinguished himself by refusing to produce the annual Fascist opus that was required by the heads of the party. Instead he had directed a movingly artistic version of *I Promessi Sposi*, long-winded and, as he himself said, "like a lead weight on the stomach", but which had the virtue of being classically comparable in the Italian eye to the works of Dante and hence patriotically suitable to the authorities. The conversation was the same old thing. The latest atrocities of the Germans, the aggravatingly slow advance of the Allies or the progress of the Anti-Fascist factions. Suddenly the telephone rang and Mario went to answer it. In the lull that followed there was a whoop from the hall. Mario re-entered the room walking on his hands, red wine spurting from his mouth onto the carpet.

"Mussolini has been ousted!" he howled. "Badoglio has taken over the government!"

From the street came the sound of horns and whistles and automobiles came screaming up the street of the Fascist Martyrs sounding their klaxons. We were stunned and then delirium set in. We drank and we talked. We felt free and exultant. Our hopes soared on the balloon of the tidings. We envisioned the end of the war for us and we drew up a list of the individuals upon whom we would soon be taking our revenge. The night passed and with the dawn a cold splinter of uncertainty began to creep in. Somehow it didn't seem wise to go all-out yet. As I stepped out into the street I noticed that the name on the corner had been changed. It read "viale Germanico".

Time passed and it was September, 1939. A Saturday evening and as usual we were dancing in the garden of the Quiriniale Hotel. All of a sudden the lights went out – we were at war.

Sandro was recalled into the airforce and stationed at Centocelle, the military airport outside Rome. His commanding officer, Beppe Candei, with his wife Adelina came often to our home in the evening. She was a provincial little thing who didn't have much to say for herself. It was obvious that she was passionately in love with her husband and she seemed emotionally incapable of being interested in anything else. They were cousins and when they fell in love the Church was against their marriage, so they ran away and spent the night together in a hotel so that their families had to allow them to marry. Every night she would sit in a corner and watch her husband, scarcely speaking to anyone, although I tried my best to draw her out and get her to join in the dancing. She either couldn't or wouldn't participate and came to life only when Beppe spoke to her. I thought her boring and tiresome and I wondered how Beppe, who appeared to be so charming and at ease, could put up with her. They had both witnessed the charming scene Sandro had created on the evening of his birthday and so I felt somewhat uncomfortable around them.

About this time a friend gave me a schnauzer puppy. I was overjoyed and loved the little animal and even Sandro couldn't object to my taking him out for short airings. So he became a symbol of liberation for me. His name was Tito, after the Roman emperor! A few days later while I was on my way to the Borghese gardens with Tito I ran into Beppe. We stopped to chat; he asked how I was and thanked me for the "pleasant" evening. His manner was restrained and as I turned to go he said, "Please excuse me, signora, but none of us could help but overhear the unfortunate scene the other night. I want you to know that we all felt very deeply for you. I don't think your husband made many friends by his behavior." I couldn't think of any reply. I mumbled something about "it didn't really matter" and we said goodbye. But all the way home I thought of Beppe's remark and somehow it made me feel better. I was late for lunch and Sandro was waiting for me.

"Where have you been?" he pounced on me as I was halfway through the door.

"Taking Tito for a walk," I said defiantly. He looked at me suspiciously but didn't pursue the matter and the subject was dropped before I had a chance to mention my encounter with Beppe. I felt guilty, but after all I had nothing to hide, or so I thought. When Sandro came home that evening, all hell broke loose. "You were seen talking to Beppe on the street this morning! Why didn't you tell me about it? What's going on between you?" The tiresome inquisition went on and on. At first I tried to defend myself and became sullen. Feelings of resentment and guilt and hatred boiled up inside me until I thought I would choke. That night he tried to make love to me and when I turned away in disgust the whole business about my encounter with Beppe started over. To him there was only one explanation for why I didn't want his embraces. But the antagonism and bitterness I felt toward him had gone too far. I didn't have the courage to deny him physically, but from that night on I led two separate and distinct lives. My emotions withdrew into a world of their own and I tried to divorce my body from all physical sensations.

Several days later I again encountered Beppe on the street and this time he invited me to have a glass of vermouth with him at a cafe. I hesitated. The fight with Sandro had put my "relationship" with Beppe in a new light. I couldn't be sure that our meeting was entirely accidental and I didn't know if I could maintain a casual attitude with Sandro's accusations in the back of my mind. Beppe sensed my indecision for he said, "My wife is shopping near here and is supposed to meet me at noon. I know she will be delighted to have you join us." Remembering her behavior at the party and the glowering looks she had cast every time he talked to some woman I doubted that, but I accepted. We sat at a little table on the sidewalk and watched the busy life of the piazza and gradually my unease evaporated. Beppe was an easy person to talk to. His life as an air force captain had taken him to many parts of the world and given him a deep understanding. He too chafed under the insularity of the Fascist regime and I found myself speaking freely, as I had never dared before. I felt happier than I had in months to have someone to talk to. Just for a moment the cloud of loneliness lifted. Adelina didn't arrive. It grew late and I knew that Sandro would be waiting at home. The thought brought a wave of apprehension. Hurriedly, I rose to go, untangled the puppy and dashed off toward home.

I could see that another scene was in the making as soon as I opened the door.

"Where have you been?" In a flash I weighed the pros

and cons. Someone was sure to have seen us sitting in front of the cafe, but I knew that Sandro would never believe that Adelina was supposed to join us. I decided to take a chance.

"I'm sorry to be late, Sandro," I said. "I was shopping and I walked farther than I realized and then I couldn't take a bus on account of the dog."

He looked at me suspiciously. "Did you meet anyone?" he asked.

I felt myself get hot all over. "No," I lied. The incident passed and I prayed that I would get away with it. I spent a miserable afternoon cooped up in the house. At four in the evening, Sandro phoned and asked me to meet him at Venchi's, a little bar on the via Veneto where our crowd met frequently for an aperitif before going on for dinner. I got there early and Beppe and Adelina were at the bar. I was sitting with them when Sandro arrived. To my surprise, he greeted them both cordially and we ended up dining together. Afterwards we went dancing. For some reason I felt safe with Beppe; I was sure that Sandro would not make a scene in front of him so I allowed myself two dances. As we returned to our table after the last dance Beppe asked me if I would meet him the next morning at the same cafe. I laughed, but gave no definite answer. As we said goodnight he whispered, "I'll be waiting at noon."

I didn't sleep much that night. I wanted to meet Beppe but I was frightened. I had the feeling that Sandro was driving me into something and that there would be no turning back once I had given in. By morning I was still undecided, and then in a moment of recklessness I gave in. When Beppe arrived at noon I was waiting for him.

Then began weeks of intrigue and subterfuge. At first I met Beppe only for an hour in the morning and then rushed home with my heart pounding, to be there before Sandro arrived for lunch. I began to live for those stolen hours and I knew I was falling in love, but I didn't care and I refused to think of the outcome. We talked for hours and I poured out my loneliness, my disappointment in my marriage, my sense of having failed. Beppe, in a strange way, restored some of my faith in myself.

When France fell I was so shocked and horrified that I could no longer keep my anti-Fascist opinions to myself and Sandro warned me that I was heading for trouble unless I shut up. He had gradually been working his way up in the Party and was beginning to feel very insecure with an American wife. It was this fear, I think, which made him decide to go to a Party meeting in Turin to which he obviously couldn't take me. It would be the first time since we had been married that I had been left alone and I was in a fever of anticipation. I couldn't eat or sleep with excitement and worry that something might come up to prevent the trip. The morning he left I called Beppe and we arranged to be together that afternoon. We met at an apartment he had borrowed from a friend. At first I felt awkward. We had never really been alone together, but gradually the tension eased. Sandro was far away, my sense of responsibility towards him had long since vanished. There was nothing in my thoughts but Beppe. All the months of frustration and waiting, the stealthy meetings and terror of being discovered climaxed on that afternoon when we became lovers. I had no feelings of guilt, I felt renewed and strengthened. The physical intimacy had merely reinforced my love and I hugged this secret to my heart as if it could wipe out all the bitterness. The afternoon ended on a comic note. As we were getting dressed we heard a key turning in the lock. "Oh, *mio dio*," exclaimed Beppe. "It must be late and my friend will be returning!" In a flash we made for the window – fortunately we were on the ground floor – and scrambled out. Anticlimax!

The day before Sandro was due to return we were having a last drink in the apartment. We had talked of Sandro and my life with him and Beppe was telling me something about Adelina. Theirs was a strange relationship. They had grown up together in a little town in the Veneto region. She had hero-worshipped him through school and their families were close. Then came the runaway marriage and Beppe's assignment to Rome. "Why haven't you any children, Beppe?" I asked. "If Adelina had a family perhaps she would cling to you less. She doesn't seem to be able to make friends and it must be lonely for her."

He hesitated. "I will tell you something in strict confidence," he said. "I am sterile. Adelina doesn't know it. She thinks it is she who can't have children. I can't bring myself to tell her the truth. Perhaps some day…"

I didn't know what to say. It was none of my affair and I didn't particularly care for Adelina anyway. Besides, with Sandro due to return I was much too concerned with when we could meet again and how I was going to work it out. "When will I see you again, Beppe?" I asked. "It won't be easy once Sandro is back, but I'll try to manage somehow."

"I'm afraid it can't be for a few weeks, *cara*," he said gently. "I didn't want to spoil our week by telling you before, but I am going to Tripoli. I have to deliver a plane and I don't know how long it will be before I can get back. I have just been waiting in Rome for reassignment and now that we are at war I can't make plans."

I was dumbfounded. I felt as if the only security I had to cling to was being snatched from me. How could I face Sandro unless I knew that Beppe was somewhere near! All my assurance was gone and I could only stare at him unhappily, while my heart filled with dread. "Oh Beppe, *tesoro*!" I burst out. "You can't leave me now. I've been so happy for the first time in so long. This war – what will it do to us?" I knew it was no use.

He took my face in his hands. "It won't be for long, I'll be back soon. We have had so little time. If we had only found each other sooner…"

"I know," I said. "I won't make it hard for you. Will you write to me – to Poste Restante? Then Sandro won't find out." We kissed. I went home and went to my room. I couldn't afford to cry. Sandro was arriving early in the morning and he would be sure to notice. I lay on the bed and waves of nausea swept over me. I felt as if I was falling into a pit, the floor, the whole room seemed to drop from under me. I finally fell asleep with the light on and when I awoke it was daylight and Sandro was standing in the room beside the bed.

Then began the most agonizing two weeks of my life. I haunted the Poste Restante window at San Silvestro, the general post office. My morning walks with the puppy consisted of a wild taxi ride to the Post and back before Sandro came home. Outwardly, I suppose, I must have appeared as usual since our life went on as before. My husband found nothing to complain about. After my morning outing I was content to stay home – with Beppe's letters. They were wonderful letters. They told of his love for me and relived the short week we had had together. I read and memorized them and then I tore them into small pieces and burned them. Then one morning I found one that said he was coming back. All that day my heart sang. Life had started again. Beppe was coming home. I could face any problem once he was with me again. After dinner Sandro and I sat listening to the news on the radio. Among the war bulletins was the announcement of the crash of a plane on a routine flight from Tripoli. Among the list of passengers was Beppe's name.

Somehow I got through that night and the day that followed. I couldn't allow myself to think. Sandro must never suspect that what I felt was any deeper than the usual grief at the loss of a casual friend. Two days passed and the strain was becoming almost more than I could bear. Then we had a telephone call. It was from the landlady of Beppe's apartment. She was almost incoherent, but we gathered that Adelina had tried to commit suicide. By the time we got there she had been rushed to hospital. Sandro and I went right over. We talked to the young doctor who had taken care of her. He said that she had tried to slash her wrists but hadn't succeeded in doing too much damage, however she was in a state of shock and would have to be hospitalized for several days. There didn't seem to be much that we could do so we left word for her to call us as soon as she was able – that we would take care of her, she could stay with us. A week later she arrived and moved in. At first it was a strained relationship, but gradually the ice thawed. Adelina began to look on me as a friend, and soon we were shopping together, eating ice cream in the after-noon, talking, and it wasn't long before she confided in me that she had taken a lover. I was in a quandary. I asked her, "Are you taking precautions?"

"Oh, I don't have to," she replied. "Beppe told me I couldn't have children." I kept quiet. Should I destroy her faith in Beppe and her new-found friendship for me, or should I let nature take its course and hope for the best? I chose the latter. At heart I am a coward. However, it wasn't long before she came to me and confessed that she was pregnant. We asked around. An abortion in Catholic Italy was not an easy thing to find. We finally discovered a woman who was willing and one morning I took her – she was very sick, an infection developed, but I nursed her and we became closer than ever and Sandro never found out.

Soon after that she went to live with her sister in a little town near Genoa. Sandro and I had just returned from Budapest where he had played polo with the Italian team. On the way we had spent the night in Vienna, blacked out, but still beautiful, and had been given a special performance by the Lipizzaner stallions. Breathtaking! I was a member of the women's team, but since Sandro would not allow me to ride his horses I had to ride ones that belonged to the captain of the Italian team. They were very fast and had very hard mouths and they frequently carried me off the field and back to the barn, which was very embarrassing and ignominious.

Then, as guests of Admiral Horthy, Budapest had been ours. A whole week of being entertained with delicious food, evenings dancing the czardas at a villa on the shore of Lake Balaton – what a lovely, lovely break. Then back to Rome.

One day, returning from the polo field at Acqua Acetosa, as usual I was on my bike hanging on to Sandro's car (during wartime women were not allowed to ride in cars) when we were stopped by a policemen. "The chief wants to see you," he said. Senise? The very name sent chills down my spine. What now?

We left the car and were driven to the central police station. Senise received us at once. "You are ordered to a concentration camp near Assisi," he said coldly.

"My God! Why?" asked Sandro.

"You were seen with golf clubs in your car," he replied.

"For your information, those were polo mallets," I interjected haughtily.

"Whatever they were it is not seemly during war to entertain yourself thus. What's more, this order comes from very high."

"My child, my daughter…" I choked.

"What of her? You must make some arrangement," he said. I burst into tears, not of fear nor despair but of pure rage. Sandro hustled me out before I could say anything damaging and we went home.

Immediately I called Gemma, my dearest friend, and through my sobs explained the situation. She thought for a moment, then said, "You say he told you the command came from high up?"

"Yes," I replied.

Another silence, then she said pensively, "Riccardi!"

Flashback – there were two beautiful sisters in Rome at that time, married, one dark, Bianca, the other blonde, Diana. Bianca was Sandro's mistress, Diana was the mistress of the Minister of the Treasury, Riccardi.

"It's just an idea," said Gemma. "But do you suppose Riccardi has mixed up the sisters and wants to get rid of Sandro?" That hadn't occurred to me, but it was typical of Gemma's contorted thinking. "Why don't you contact

Ciano?" she asked. She knew that Mussolini's son-in-law had a fondness for me. "I'll bet he could squash this in a minute." It was worth trying and for once Sandro didn't object to my talking to a man without being chaperoned. I was able to arrange an audience for the next day.

Ciano seemed glad to see me. "To what do I owe this pleasure, Mara?" he asked.

"Excellency…" I began, and then I blurted out the whole sorry story and my suspicions as to the cause, that perhaps, somehow, Riccardi might be involved. He heard me out, a perplexed look on his face – and then he burst into roars of laughter. "Go home Mara," he said. "I myself will speak to Senise and straighten this out – and as to Riccardi, leave him to me. After this, though, tell your husband to be careful!"

I left. We heard no more about it.

Aftermath: When the Allies arrived and liberated Rome from the German occupiers, the first thing a mob did was storm the police station. They grabbed Senise, a woman bit his ear off, and they dumped him off a bridge into the Tiber.

Chapter II

July 17, 1942 will always remain in my memory for two reasons. In the first place it was the day on which the first bombardment of Rome took place. Fortunately, I happened to be at home that morning when the sirens went at eleven o'clock, but by that time, we in Rome were so used to false air-raid alarms that nobody bothered much about it... until the first bombs began to drop! And even then, people in the center of the city told me afterwards that they had no idea that a real bombardment had been going on. But I, who lived near the airport of Littoria, midway between it and the San Lorenzo quarter, passed, as the Italians say, *un brutto quarto d'ora*, it being my first experience. About one in the afternoon I turned on the radio to hear the news bulletin, and to my surprise heard a voice from the principal Rome station announcing that during the morning numerous bombs had been dropped on Rome and that the damage was in the process of being verified! And this while wave after wave were still passing over our heads, and at each detonation the doors and windows rattled, the house shook and a blast of cold air came in through the closed shutters. "They just couldn't wait to broadcast this," I thought. But knowing the intrepid Romans, I was surprised they managed to get anyone to stand up before the microphone! Naturally, the other Italian cities rejoiced, as Rome's immunity had long been a source of malcontent, envy, and ill-natured gibes... Not without reason. About two in the afternoon we watched the last wave of elongated, silvery forms disappear into the distant clouds, and when the all clear sounded I started frantically to try to retrace my small daughter who, in the meantime, had been at large with her governess. Naturally, I imagined that they were in some innocuous place such as the Borghese gardens enjoying the fresh air in comparative safety so it was to my annoyance to hear the governess's voice gibbering over the telephone from San Giovanni, where they had passed the last three hours in a cellar, two hundred feet from where one of the three bombs that were dropped on that quarter had fallen. When they at last arrived home, five-year-old Giulia was much the more calm of the two, so I never did find out the reason for that mysterious morning excursion.

Everybody stuck pretty close to home during the afternoon and after dinner we had another alarm, but fortunately this time nothing came of it. I got to bed at a fairly early hour and had just gotten to sleep when the governess erupted into the room and with staring eyes announced that the portiere had been warned by the U.N.P.A. (the Italian equivalent of air-raid wardens) that a munitions train was about to blow up at the airport and our entire quarter had been ordered to evacuate. Still half asleep I sprang out of bed, but not putting too much faith in the governess's assertions I decided to find out first just how serious the situation was. The first person I ran into was my next-door neighbor who confirmed the report, saying he had already telephoned the fascist headquarters and the speedier and further the removal the better. While I was talking in the doorway the governess and the child shot past me, neither fully dressed, like something from a Mickey Mouse cartoon, and shouting to them to wait for me in the street I went back to hurry the two maids. Without stopping to dress I threw on a wrapper, switched off the gas and electricity and with the two women following me I hurried down the steps. No Giulia, no Signorina and no sign of life anywhere in the street. We walked up the block to the square taking turns calling, but with no result. In the meantime other houses had begun to disgorge disgruntled inhabitants in various stages of undress, and the Piazza was soon swarming with old and young, baby carriages and grandmothers, men with lap-robes and suitcases, some fully dressed, but the majority as defenseless against the damp Roman night as I was. For while the days may be scorching in summer, at night there comes a mist up from the Tiber and the thermometer takes a noticeable drop.

The main idea seemed to be to reach Villa Borghese for safety, so we followed along, at intervals calling for Giulia, but despairing of finding her among so many people. We reached the Borghese gardens after about a quarter of an hour's walk, and there we encountered more people, all milling around uncertainly and still they came until there must have been two or three thousand standing about or sitting on the damp grass under the trees. Presently, my little group was augmented by the staff, husband and wife, of other tenants in our apartment building, who had become separated from their friends and were looking for a nucleus to which to attach themselves. We footed it as far as the tram lines to see if any trains were running, or at least to find some informed person to tell us what to do, because the strange characteristic of that adventure was the complete absence of authority in any form. Not a black shirt, policeman or carabiniere was to be found. Just thousands of people wandering from place to place exchanging rumors and nobody really knowing what it was all about.

I began to get exasperated and my feet were starting to hurt and the more I considered it, the less attractive began to appear a night under a tree with no blankets. So I cautioned my party of my maid and cook – a corpulent soul whose feet had shown signs of collapsing even before mine – and the other couple, to remain where they were while I went back to the local fascist house to see if I could obtain any information.

Piazza Ungheria presented the same wild appearance as earlier. More and more people were continually arriving, milling about in the bright moonlight, and I fought my way through them to the Fascio where others were already gathering. The scene there was even less encouraging. There seemed to be no official in charge, and when I finally buttonholed an individual in uniform and demanded particulars he replied, "I don't know any more than you. We have received orders to clear this area of people within a range of three kilometers. If you want to be safe you must get to the other side of the Borghese. If not, go back to sleep!" This was discouraging as I had encountered people in "the Borghese" coming from the opposite side of Rome who had received the same instructions! However, there was no use in arguing so I traipsed back to my little group patiently encamped by the side of the road and imparted my news finishing with, "If it wasn't for the fact that my child is at large, I don't know where or with whom or how equipped, I, personally, would go back to bed. However, I cannot be responsible for sending you home in case something should happen. So everyone had better choose for himself." After quite a discussion it was decided that Alberta, my maid, and I should return home, get dressed, pack a bag with emergency rations, and on the way glean what news there was to be had. The others would return to the square to wait for us.

The house was deserted, the portiere had fled with all the others, and I can assure you we lost no time in assembling the necessary equipment and escaping. I brought along two blankets as a precaution, fortunate, as we found poor Ada, the cook, sitting in the middle of the tramlines swearing she would rather be blown up than move another step. I, just for the hell of it, decided to make one more trip to the Fascio before settling down for the night, or rather morning, as it was now close on four o'clock, so I tottered off. Arriving at the entrance I found it jammed by a group of people all congratulating each other at the danger past and preparing to go home. This seemed too good to be true so I pushed inside and sure enough, I was told, "False alarm, exaggeration, return to your homes!"

At that I burst out, "And all those poor people in the Villa Borghese, at least send somebody to let them know. You can't let them stay out all night in the cold for no reason!" A shrug of the shoulders. Declaiming loudly the inefficiency of fascist organizations when it was most needed, I made my way down the stairs and, after announcing the latest decision to my satellites, we picked up our bundles and trailed wearily homeward before another order should arrive to send us back into the bush.

The first thing I heard on entering the house was the telephone ringing. I rushed to answer and heard the voice of my top-floor neighbor. "Signora, we found your governess racing up the street dragging the baby behind her half dressed, and as we had a taxi we picked them up and brought them with us to spend the night with some friends in the center of town. Giulia is safe and asleep." Speechless, I sent my thanks and, advising a dose of bromide for the governess, I rang off. It was just five in the morning.

The next day the munitions train was blown up bit by bit, but I doubt if anybody was the wiser except the persons actually involved!

About the middle of August, I found the city heat too much for me, and so when I started dreaming at night of bathing in the emerald waters off Brioni, and swimming after elusive fish through cool submarine depths, I decided to decamp. The government had changed from Fascist to Militarist. But aside from fiery articles in the newspapers there was no appreciable difference. The war, if such it could be called from an Italian point of view, dragged monotonously on. Everyone was sticking pretty close to home in anticipation of unforeseen events, and most people's villeggiatura had gone by the board. However, it was not yet too late in the season for good bathing. So I selected Monte Circeo, a rocky promontory about fifty miles from Rome, said to be the site of Circe's cave and an excellent spot for fishing with the underwater gun.

I left early one morning with my small daughter Giulia and two friends, both fishing enthusiasts, and we arrived after an agonizing journey of five hours to cover the bare sixty kilometers. Circeo was heavenly. The hotel, set on a peak of rock overlooking the rugged shoreline, was empty except for three other clients. We had a delightful swim and decided immediately to stay as long as the weather held out instead of the prescribed weekend.

The days drifted lazily by, what with bathing, row-boating and acting in a haphazard fashion as governess to Giuli, until one evening we were standing on the terrace watching a full moon rise out of the sea when we heard shouts in the distance coming from a huddle of fishermen's cottages. They came nearer and nearer and we were able to distinguish the words "ARMISTICE! ARMISTICE!" Scarcely believing our ears and half afraid that it would prove to be just another of the many rumors that materialized from time to time, we hurried towards the sounds and met a group of fishermen coming from the cove. Yes, it was true! Yes, Marshal Badoglio had announced it over the radio in the eight-thirty broadcast. (Our hotel radio had been out of order since the first day of our arrival). "And the Germans?" was our first question. Oh, the Germans will have to leave, the Marshal had cautioned the soldiers to be ready to take up arms again against "another" enemy. Everything was very simple. Tonight the Rome airports will be occupied by Allied planes, and tomorrow the English will land under our very noses and life will at once return to normal after the due period of frenzied rejoicing! It sounded impossible, too good to be true. Armistice! Before going to bed that night I strolled outside to have a last look at the moon on the water, and to see if I could distinguish any of the myriads of planes that had been roaring overhead. Out of the dusk had materialized a truck full of Germans who were silently picketing the hotel. Renouncing my intention of communing with the night, I hurriedly retired, my faith in the armistice a bit shaken.

The next day dawned hot and sunny. My friends and I were determined to return to Rome at all costs. We couldn't bear the thought of missing any excitement that happened to be going, and besides, the idea of remaining in such an out-of-the-way place with no hope of news, cut off from radio and telephone, was intolerable. We ordered a small cart to take us the fifteen miles to the station (we had buried the car to prevent it from being requisitioned by the Germans) and the four of us piled on with our luggage, the driver being forced to sit on one of the shafts at my feet. We hoped to get to Terracina for the twelve-thirty train to Rome, and we started off early in high spirits. It promised to be a glorious day, and who knew what adventures lay before us? Our first check occurred when we met a group of peasants who told us that the road to Terracina was closed as the English were already in the harbor and landing troops. We decided to go on, as even if it were true I felt that I would rather cope with the English any day than the Germans. To make sure, however, we stopped a German truck and were informed that there was no truth to the rumor. After having collected a series of contradictory reports, all of which tallied, however, on the detail that Terracina was closed to transit, we changed our route somewhat and headed for a way station in a small town on the other side of the via Appia. By this time the first fine careless rapture had subsided. The sun was scorching, the seat was hard, and we were running out of cigarettes. At one point we trotted through a shady side road which brought some relief, but also contributed swarms of horse flies to our discomfiture.

We crossed the via Appia after making a considerable detour to avoid some mined bridges, and were within a few miles of our goal, when we were stopped by a carload of refugees who told us that on no account was it possible to travel by train! Most of them had stopped running and the remaining few had been commandeered by the German forces. This was something we hadn't counted on. Disconsolately, we turned back to via Appia and stopped near a power station, beside which was a soldiers' barrack. Here at last we can get some definite information, we thought. We got out to stretch our legs and our friendly driver succeeded in borrowing an armful of forage for the pony before going off to find the officer in charge. This individual turned out to be a young lieutenant who, we soon realized, was even more bewildered than we were. "We have no orders," he said. "The Rome radio has not broadcast at all so far today, and some say that the station has been seized by the Germans. Terracina has been evacuated. We saw the camions go by early this morning. Trains? No, I think there will be no trains for some time."

"What will you do?" I asked.

"I don't know," he admitted. "Some of the soldiers are already out of uniform. They have one idea only – to get home." He also told us that if we were lucky enough to come across a military vehicle, they had orders to pick up civilians, but since we knew that Terracina had been emptied and the town closed to further traffic, there seemed little hope of encountering anything going in our direction, towards Rome. We waited around for almost an hour in a terrible state of indecision. To go back to Circeo to be stuck for heaven knew how long seemed too heartbreaking. My friend was all for striking out on foot, but with a five-year-old child I couldn't dare risk it. At last, however, she and her companion decided to undertake the journey, and after despoiling me of the lunch basket they set briskly off and I was left gazing somewhat forlornly after their retreating figures. As it turned out, they were able to obtain a lift from some Germans after only a few kilometers and were in Rome that same evening, but not knowing this, I wasted much time worrying over their fate in the days that followed.

After waiting some time on the off chance of hailing a passing car, I finally got discouraged. The long straight road stretched emptily in either direction, and I reluctantly turned my face seaward. The three-hour ride back was a nightmare. I felt my unprotected face frizzling in the sun, the pangs of hunger grew sharper, and poor little Giuli was more and more restless. As a final indignity, I burned off all my eyelashes while trying to light a cigarette with a horse blanket over my head so as to be sure of not wasting the last match! We arrived back at the hotel in the late afternoon tired, hungry, and uncertain as to the future.

Then began a week of interminable waiting filled with false rumors and futile conjectures. Of the few troops that had been stationed in the vicinity, the officers were the first to shed their uniforms and throw aside their arms. The soldiers soon followed suit, and spent their time bathing and dynamiting fish for something to eat. The ammunition and grenades that had been left carelessly thrown down ended up in the hands of the small village boys, causing us all much nervous anxiety. Bit by bit, the Germans took over the countryside. There were tales of fighting in nearby towns, but resistance was soon found to be useless. The Italian radio was still silent. The soldiers skulked about by day out of sight of the Germans and by night kindly peasants and villagers gave them food and a place to sleep. All had but one thought – to get home – and, alone and in groups, they wandered off, on foot, on bicycles and in carts. The officers were not so much to blame as might seem at first. After that last broadcast announcing the armistice and charging the soldiers to lay down their arms, but to be ready to pick them up again, there had been no further orders. Each officer found himself solely responsible for his own unit, with no way of appealing to a higher command or knowing what his brother officers were doing. Each one interpreted the situation as he thought best, and some held out as long as their equipment permitted, while others surrendered, saving what they could. And in the meantime, there was no news from Rome. We did not know if the capital was in Italian, English or German hands, if there was fighting or not. And still no trains. The days passed, sunny and calm. No news filtered in to depress or rejoice our little community. The few of us who were, as we felt, trapped in the hotel, formulated and discarded wild plans of escape, although we all realized that a situation more fortunate than ours would be difficult to find. We were well housed, clothed and fed. We were free to bathe and ramble about with no curfew to bother us, and the few troops that had taken over paid little attention to our small point of the promontory. It was the lack of news and action that was maddening. That and not knowing how long the situation was to continue.

At last, on the ninth day, my husband turned up in our car. How he managed to obtain a German pass and the three false starts he had made to come and rescue us were recounted with dramatic details. The situation in Rome was worse than we had expected. The city had capitulated immediately and although the Germans had more or less calmed down by now it was still fairly dangerous to circulate. The spasmodic Italian defiances were severely punished. Our peaceful Circe's rock seemed a haven by comparison. However, we thought it best to get back while the permit for the car was still valid.

The drive back was like something from a Hemingway novel. The roads on each side were lined with soldiers and more soldiers. In various stages of undress, some of them shoeless, some with bandaged feet, some in pushcarts, they plodded on, heading north, heading south. I imagined all the roads taken over by this tragic procession, and thought of the many big words and false hopes that had led to such a debacle. Surely such treachery would not go unpunished. As far as the eye could see it unwound and each curve brought into sight a repetition of the one before. With faces hopelessly set, grimly struggling on mile after heartbreaking mile, the ex-Italian army was returning home.

We arrived in Rome after our disastrous ride from Terracina to find the city in a complete state of chaos. (I must make a parenthesis here, which may sound premature but which struck me when, over a year later, I read in *Stars and Stripes* of the adventurous trip to Rome that two American generals took the day before the armistice, disembarking at Terracina and whisking through to Rome under my very nose! If I had only known.) The Germans were still shelling at intervals having apparently taken over the city with about 2000 men in the face of an entire Italian armored division, and rumors were flying, contradictory and all unflattering to the Italians. Food was non-existent. None was coming in. The markets were all closed and few people dared to circulate. Everyone was waiting for the next move. No one dared talk to his neighbor, which made for an appalling lack of organization. Looking back now one can say – that was the moment to have done this or that; the first days would have been ideal for going through the lines and many profited. One by one people faded out of the picture and the Jewish population became more and more nervous as restrictions were clamped down on its shops, restaurants and other activities – but as yet nothing was organized.

When my husband suggested that it might be better to go into hiding I first laughed at the idea and then got angry when I realized that he was thinking seriously. I simply couldn't figure out why. On the assumption that I was a close relative of the President of the United States the order had gone out for my removal to Germany as a hostage. I thought that was funny, as I knew no one would put up a nickel to rescue an Oyster Bay or out-of-season Roosevelt. I had imagined that the boring presence of the war would drag itself out just as well under the German occupation as under the Fascist regime. As yet, I had not had much traffic with our occupiers and knowing the Italians I thought they were always inclined to take things too intensely anyway. However, I was rushed into it before I had much time to think. It seemed to me a most undignified undertaking but I comforted myself with the thought that at most it was a question of a few days. The Salerno beach head was proceeding, Montgomery's forces had just linked up with 5th Army, the fall of Naples seemed to be imminent, and then we figured that the march on Rome could take only about a week. At the most by the middle of October – I thought, how ironic to have Rome fail on the twenty-eighth anniversary of the Fascist march to Rome! It was probably just as well that I didn't realize that I was in for nine long, weary, comfortless months of terror and seclusion.

We got to work right away disposing of our valuables. My jewelry, American passport and about one hundred thousand lire in bills were locked in an old cashbox and hurriedly, secretly buried by night in my father-in-law's garden and a bed of lettuce sown over. Our clothes, silver and other portable objects of value were sealed in boxes and walled up in an empty apartment rented under fictitious names by a trusted friend who was to act as liaison with us and the outside world. Everything was ready. I sent my little daughter to stay with her grandmother and one evening my husband and I climbed into a taxi with a couple of handbags, having first bought tickets for Milan, and had ourselves driven to the station. From that moment – September 15 – until Rome was liberated by the Allies the following year in June, we were as much lost to sight as if we had died and been buried. The fact of our going to Milan leaked out, of course on purpose, and so everybody figured that we had escaped across the Swiss border. Instead we doubled back from the station and made our way on foot down the via di Porta Maggiore to an apartment building near the city gates. Watching our chance when the portiere wasn't looking, we sneaked up the stairs to a small flat, which had been prepared for us.

Our days fell quickly into a routine. I had never been much of a housewife or cook and at first it took me hours to prepare our simple meals; the housework tired me out so that at least I could sleep at night. What little food and news we got was brought by our trustworthy friend. Coffee was brought in the raw bean. So first it had to be roasted in a kind of sieve over a gas flame before being ground. Soon there was no more coffee, just some kind of ersatz bean that looked like an acorn so I soon eliminated that chore. I seem to have spent a great deal of time sprinkling eggplant slices with rock salt and then pressing them between weights. The resultant liquid was considered by the Italians to be poisonous and was poured off before the eggplant was fried. I always started the actual frying with great enthusiasm. The thin slices sizzled and smelled as if I were a REAL cook, but invariably when half done the pressure of the gas would drop and everything would just float about in the grease, the eggplant and potatoes all swimming around together like fat worms. It was even worse when we fell heir to a piece of meat, usually a large veal roast. There was no refrigerator, but there were plenty of ants. They crawled all over the kitchen. I found that the only way I could keep them out of the food was to put a saucer of water under each table leg. One day I got the brilliant idea that if water would keep the ants off the meat why not just keep the meat right in the water? I filled the kitchen sink and put the roast in and would slice a bit off for each meal. On the third day, my husband began sniffing at the food and saying it didn't taste right. But he was finicky anyway so I told him he didn't have to eat it if he didn't want to, but that was all there was and if he wanted to help with the cooking, he was welcome. He tracked the smell down to the meat, fast disintegrating in its tub of water, so my short cut to housekeeping was short lived.

Usually he spent his time with his ear glued to the radio following the war news from BBC broadcasts and we marked the Allied advances on an old automobile map that we found in a guide to Italy. I called that map our Via Crucis, I still have it today, and how we agonized over it as our armies inched their way up the peninsula. Occasionally, our friend would come to bring us news of the outside world and replenish our larder. He had friends upstairs whom he was accustomed to visit, so his comings and goings were not suspect: also it was one way of keeping tabs on whether or not our presence had been noticed. It is hard to live for months trying to be not only invisible but also inaudible. We could not take baths – the sound of running water coming from a deserted apartment would have been highly suspicious, and besides the gas was too feeble to heat it: the radio had to be turned down so that it was barely audible except right up close, we walked in our bare feet and took extreme care opening and closing doors. Since the building was built with all the plumbing facilities and piping in the same locations it was no trick to flush the toilet. Whenever someone in an apartment above us flushed, one of us would rush to flush, the noise was so obvious. Anyway, like all Italian plumbing circa 1930 that for all anyone could tell it could have been one toilet or ten.

Occasionally, we would have the disquieting news that the Germans were putting dragnets around the houses in our block aside from picking people off the streets, and it had gotten so that only the very young or the very old ventured out. There were few houses in Rome at that time that didn't have a walled-up room containing valuables or an enforced guest of some type, boys of military age, Allied prisoners of war, people on the German-Fascist blacklist. After a while they got wise to the blocked off room idea and would visit the various apartments with a floor plan in hand. More and more restrictions were being enforced – black marketeering was punishable by death, there was a 9 p.m. curfew and all men born between 1921 and 1925 were being shang-haied for "Labor Service", whatever that meant. A priest had been shot in front of the altar of Santa Maria Maggire just down the street from our building. The German soldier who did it said he thought it was a partisan masquerading as a priest. The constant anxiety worked on our nerves and at every commotion in the street we would run to the windows to peer fearfully from behind the curtains. Aside from that we started getting little sleep as the Allies had begun to bomb the airfields at night and there were two not very far from our house. There was no question of going to a shelter, as we would only advertise our presence. The quarter we lived in had been quite well bombed already, as it was far enough out to come within range of the planes aiming for Centocelle airfield, and so we played pinochle and drank up all the wine we could find. Fortunately, the former tenants were pretty well stocked and there was no fear of their walking in on us as they were in the south and therefore already in liberated Italy. Time dragged on like this for almost two months and every day our hope of seeing an end grew less sanguine. The farce of Rome being an "open city" and the constant trickle of news about German atrocities began to take a back seat to my own personal problems. I blamed my husband for not having arranged to try to get through the lines as so many had done in the first days of confusion, and he blamed me for being American, and looking it! One reason for the disgusting set-up in Rome was the fact that we were always going to be "liberated". No one thought that it would take so long, and while in the north the partisans sensibly settled down for a long siege and organized themselves against the Germans, in Rome people figured it was simpler to hide until the occupation blew over without doing anything to help it on its way. So, they armed themselves and holed up and passed time organizing political parties that talked very big but never showed up in moments of crisis. We figured that the sub rosa population of Rome had increased the city's citizenry by about 300,000.

One day towards the end of October our friend arrived looking very worried. He had seen my mother-in-law and she had told him that the Fascist authorities had been to our home looking for us. She had stalled them and after they left had smuggled our child out of the house and to the home of a friend. We looked at each other blankly. This was something we had hardly bargained for and I cursed myself for my carelessness. We all knew of the German mania for hostages, but I stupidly hadn't thought they would seek a five-year-old child. Coincidence... I was to learn differently the next day. Our friend left and promised to keep us informed and for the next week we ransacked our brains and explored every avenue of escape, hashed over every possible solution. The next morning, however, a battering on the door awakened me; of course we didn't dare open it, but in the street opposite was a SS truck. I stood behind the door and listened to the German voices, then I heard someone speaking Italian and the portiere answering. They asked after a family who lived in the building and I could tell it was a Jewish name. The portiere replied that they lived in the apartment above us. At least they weren't after us this time. I went back to the window taking care not to be seen and soon the soldiers emerged in frustration – evidently the family they sought had already fled. A week later our friend came back with more bad news. Giulia had been discovered. Apparently the nurse, warned by the portiere, had spirited her out of the house as the SS came up the stairs. Something had to be done. A convent seemed to be the only solution – if we could find one to take us in, as they were almost all full of refugees. It was decided I would go with the child and my husband made arrangements to hide out in the Vatican; this was for me the final degradation – the ultimate act of cowardice, and the act which finally and forever broke whatever ties there had been between us. I also found myself almost resenting my daughter who was tying me down and preventing at least a try for the other side of the lines where I could join my own people. That my husband didn't immediately strike out for the hills and join the partisans was something I never forgave.

At last it was all arranged. The mother house of the convent of the Sacred Heart at the end of the via Nomentana near the railroad yards accepted Giulia and me. I was provided with false documents; Margherita Roero, born in Asti, married to Capt. Alessandro Palmieri, address via Achille Grandi – a location carefully chosen since it was completely bombed out. The move was to be made just after nightfall and before curfew. Getting there was risky. All motor vehicles had either been commandeered or forcibly registered by order of Kesselring. I had only one small suitcase, but I didn't dare run the risk of walking from one end of Rome to the other for fear of being stopped by the police. A friend chanced driving me and so I left my husband to be reunited with my daughter and for the first time in six weeks I walked out of the front door. It was already dark, seven in the evening of November 2, 1943, the day the Italian Catholics call "the day of the dead."

Mrs. Margaret Roosevelt Pallavicini and daughter Julia, six years old, cousins to President and Mrs. Roosevelt, are shown in Rome hotel after hiding from Nazis for months in convent. Her husband, Alessandro Pallavicini, is Italian film producer.

Top left: Giuli aged four.
Top right: 'Mrs. Margaret Roosevelt Pallavicini and daughter Julia, six years old, cousins to President and Mrs. Roosevelt, are shown in Rome hotel after hiding from Nazis for months in convent. Her husband, Alessandro Pallavicini, is an Italian film producer.'
Bottom: Ron and me at Tony's on our return from Boston.

Top: Giuli and Randy dancing at their wedding.
Bottom: Robbie — looking oh so British naval.

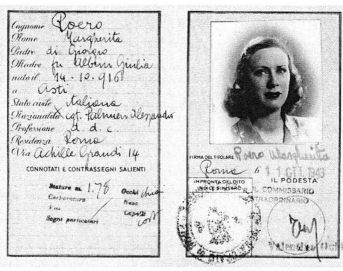

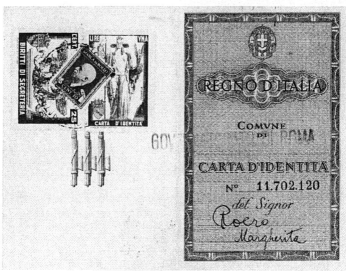

Top and bottom: My false ID.

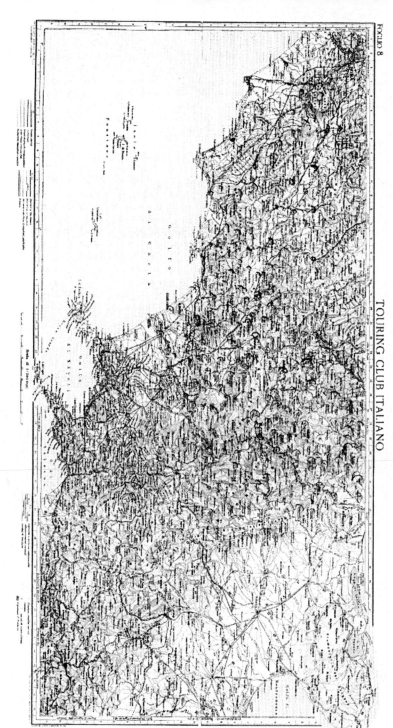

TOURING CLUB ITALIANO

My Via Crucis with each town underlined as the Allies moved up the Peninsula.

Chapter III

The convent was a large, rambling building set in a garden on the outskirts of the city. It was after dusk when I arrived but I remember being stopped by a wrought iron gate and then a gravel drive to the front door where I was deposited with my suitcase. The Mother Porter let me in and without any question or comment went to fetch Mother Perry, an elderly wizened Englishwoman with a kind, serene face who greeted me cordially and showed me to a little room on the top floor. It was so small that there was just enough space for two cots, a prie-dieu and a writing table. It overlooked the courtyard and the cloistered wing of the building and the principal advantage seemed to be that the kitchen chimney passed close to one wall. Evidently, the architect had taken that into account, as there was no radiator.

Giulia was brought to me just before supper time. She looked so strange, as if I had never seen her before, and she was shy. We felt wary of each other, I guess; too much had happened in too short a time. We descended the curved staircase hand in hand to the great marble entrance hall and were shown into a small reception room where we were to take our meals. We were both too bewildered and exhausted to eat. I am not a Roman Catholic and had never before been in contact with anyone closely connected with the Church. I was awed and uncertain as to how to behave. I knew that perhaps my very life depended upon the goodwill of the sisters and I resolved to be as unobtrusive and adaptable as possible.

I took Giulia up to our room and put her to bed and as I looked at her sleeping in the little cot a wave of tenderness swept over me and I started to cry. She seemed very dear after two months' separation and the anxieties concerning her. The future still looked dreary and hopeless and uncertain, but the Germans hadn't gotten us yet and we were together!

For the first few days I just walked in the garden, turning my face to the sun, playing with Giuli, getting to know the nuns. Reverend Mother Datti was the Superior, but she was ill and cloistered and I never saw her. Mother Perry was English, an older woman who took me under her wing with kindness and understanding. My special friend became Mother Hermans, a Belgian and one of the most beautiful women I have ever seen. She had large brown eyes and lovely teeth, a sly sense of humor and, like all the Sacred Heart nuns, was a teacher. Then of course there were the sisters who did the manual labor – the two we got to know best were sister Parisani, a gay Italian girl, and Sœur Marie. I say Sœurmarie because in my mind it always came out as one word. Our day began with Sœurmarie, who would bring a roll and a small cup of ground barley or acorns or whatever passed for coffee at the moment to our room at eight in the morning. We were both a little frightened of Sœurmarie – she was an ageless Frenchwoman with a dry sense of humor and a sense of duty that spared none, least of all herself. She had a finger in every pie and nothing happened within the convent walls without her knowledge. Sœurmarie was either a participant or a spectator. She loved to gossip and through her I gathered bits and crumbs of information about the other inhabitants of our little world, most of whom I never saw. She came from some small town in the south of France. Her accent was nasal and full of harsh "ng" sounds. There was a permanent drop at the end of her aquiline nose, and the coarsely knitted black shawl that she wore during the cold weather was fastened with a large, bright safety pin over her flat chest. After breakfast I set aside two hours for Giuli's schooling. She was learning to read and write and being quick and intelligent got through her assigned tasks in record time if she applied herself, but unfortunately that was rarely the case and then there would ensue a battle royal that would leave us both drained.

Over the high surrounding wall I could hear the whir of buses passing in the street, their overhead trolleys singing along the electric wires. The sound of feet and snatches of conversation crept in through the iron gates. Beyond the wall people still walked about the streets and rode their bicycles, free to come and go and see their friends, to talk to each other on the telephone. Freedom is a state of mind.

Outside the wall the incubus of the invader still persisted and although I didn't know it at the time very few people dared to circulate. Enforced labor and compulsory military service had cleaned the streets of all except the very young and the very old and even they were not immune when the Germans had need of labor. After every bombardment the shanghaiing of individuals would increase and people would be carted off in trucks to the latest scene of devastation. In the meantime I walked in the garden from dawn till dusk, ate my sparse meals and gradually the days fell into a routine governed by the convent bell and clock, which struck eight times an hour. That clock was at first one of my main sources of annoyance. Our little room was situated right under the clock tower and every time it chimed the windows rattled and the very walls seemed to vibrate. It struck the hours, quarters, halves and five minutes before every quarter hour. We were never at a loss to know what time it was! I would draw a breath of relief when twelve forty-five struck and we could settle down to a shorter series of chimes.

The convent was unheated and overcrowded. The mothers and sisters from Albano had been bombed out and were here now with us, and the few guests brought the total to eighty persons. There were ration books for only fifty and the nuns couldn't afford black-market food. So many of them were feeble or old or infirm in some way and the younger sisters were all overworked. The nearly blind ones worked in the kitchen. There was one in particular who sorted the dried lentils – practically our only staple food – and she always left in quantities of the little round rose-colored stones and the hollow shells from which the lentil worms had sucked the pulp.

It rained and rained and the convent grew damper and the nuns' breaths rose cloudily in the chapel during early morning masses. Sœurmarie developed a permanent list as arthritis began pulling down her left side and she would sidle crabwise down the corridors, hugging the wall. But the feebler and skinnier she got the more she forced herself to do. Her pale blue eyes flashed from behind her pince nez at the slightest suggestion that she rest or leave some of the heavier work to the younger sisters. She panted and struggled up the stairs carrying pails and jugs of water, and back down again with odd bits of furniture and rugs. I helped her to clear the top floor. The air raids had gotten bad and we were moving the bedridden mothers to the cellar. The rest of us could scamper into the garden or stay where we were, but the older and more useless the members of the order became the more zealously they were cared for. Sœurmarie, for one, never moved. The Mother Superior in vain tried to persuade her to abandon at least the top floor during the more severe raids, but Sœurmarie maintained that the Bon Dieu was looking after her as well in the attic as in the cellar. Finally, a convent rule was issued that everyone was to collect below stairs when the siren sounded. This irked Sœurmarie as she claimed it interfered with her work to keep running up and down the stairs, and sometimes we would have as many as twelve or fifteen alarms during the day.

When we would all gather it was a Dore-esque sight. Three small dark rooms led off the kitchen. They were windowless and the ceilings were crisscrossed with water pipes. Long benches lined the walls, and in the gloom one could feel rather than see the mass of rustling humanity, black billowing skirts giving off a faint odor of incense. Above the roar of the planes rose the chant and counter chant of the rosary. At the lines, "Pray for us now and at the hour of our death" my heart stopped for a brief moment. There was the fear that the two were about to coincide.

One morning we were gathered as usual. The raid was particularly severe and the house trembled with the vibration from hundreds of planes passing overhead. The nuns, sitting on two rows of benches facing each other, had started their litany and the *Ave Maria* from one side echoed the *Sancta Maria* from the other. At last the noise died away and we had the usual breathing space, which is like being in the center of a hurricane, before the planes come over again on the way back. In the stillness we heard the clop of a pair of wooden clogs such as the humbler sisters wore. Sœur Marie appeared in the doorway.

"Madame," she said to me, *"le bain est pret."*

My weekly bath. The sacred hot water carried up flights of stairs and dumped into the tub. My only chance not only to get clean, but to soak some of the chill out of my body. I heard the distant buzz of the returning planes…

"Oh, Sœur Marie…" I cried.

"On ne doit pas laisser refraicher l'eau." Inexorably she fixed me with her eyes, standing at the threshold and panting a little.

No, it mustn't be wasted, the precious fuel to heat the water nor the precious effort and time and thoughtfulness of Sœurmarie. Most of all, the challenge in her regard had to be answered. Rising, I followed her out of the room.

Little Mother Perry fluttered in to check on our welfare several times a week. We would carry on a bland, neutral kind of conversation – lament the slowness of the Allied advance – and she would chuckle over the expression "mopping up", which always seemed to follow the taking of a town and which she considered most inappropriate. Then she would drift off, much more preoccupied with the affairs of the convent than with anything that was taking place outside. The only thing I had to relieve the drabness and monotony of my existence was a small radio, which I had smuggled in in my suitcase. During the long evenings when I had put

Giuli to bed I would sit crouched over it trying to listen to the BBC broadcasts which I considered more reliable than our local press. My favorite program was a popular musical called *Forces Favorite* which was conducted by two chipper young girls and which had the most moving theme song; I afterward discovered it was *When You Wish Upon a Star*. To this day, if I hear it, I am transported for a moment back to that small room, and I see myself in one of my two skirts, a brown one and a green one, bundled in a sweater and coat with my head bent over the radio waiting for Jean to come on with the mysterious announcements with which the program always started and which would make me itch with curiosity.

Fortunately, one of the older nuns, Mother du Passage, offered to give Giuli French lessons. So off they would go together giving me a free hour before lunch. It was at this point that I realized that only two things were going to get me through this period and help me to retain my sanity – routine and discipline. So it was that I marked out my five-kilometer walk, which I stuck to grimly rain or shine during all the winter months in that hour before lunch. Lunch, as all our other meals, was looked forward to not so much because it was something to eat, but because it broke up the monotony of the day's routine. Rome was without salt, which could make even the most delicate cuisine rather bland. Unless my faithful friend had paid a visit bringing a bit of meat, our diet consisted of pasta made out of some kind of grain which had the consistency of sawdust and the famous lentil soup. However, as we had no ration cards there was no use complaining. After lunch I put Giuli down for a rest and sought out the company of Mother Hermans. She

loaned me books in French about the lives of the saints –
I had never dreamed there were so many nor that they all
seemed to take such a masochistic delight in hardship
and deprivation. I could not comprehend the ecstasy of
offering up one's worldly suffering to God, neither could
I understand what purpose it could serve or of what
solace it could be. Few of us achieve sainthood, but I felt
that if I could only find some plan or reason or purpose
to my present life that in any way could seem beneficial
to the good Lord I would gladly offer it up in order to
gain some peace of mind. When the lives of the saints
palled I undertook a course in philosophy with Mother
Hermans and I forced myself not to think. Discipline and
routine!

After Giulia's rest we walked again in the garden and
at four in the evening were served a cup of tea in our
little dining room before the benediction service. The
clock would strike the vesper hour at four fifteen in the
evening and from all directions the black habits with
their faint sweet odor of incense would whisk silently
toward the chapel. Giuli and I knelt in the back row on
the hard bench, bolt upright like the nuns, while the
delicate strains of *Tantum Ergo* rang out a capella from the
mezzanine and I tried not to think of how my knees hurt.
I finally had to ask permission to use a little red velvet
padded prie-dieu just at the side entrance to the chapel.
From this vantage point, I could see the altar with its
enormous candle – almost from the first days I made a
mental mark halfway down the candle and decided when
it had burned down that far *they* would arrive.

As the days grew shorter Giuli and I would go back to
our room after benediction to wait for supper. I tried to
entertain her, reading fairy stories and playing games, but

I was not very good at being with children and it was irritating for both of us. Mealtimes were almost as bad. Giuli had a picky appetite and since I realized she needed the food I would try to push it down her throat while my own mouth watered. The more I tried to force it on her the less she ate and we would end up with my being furious with frustration and hunger and poor little Giuli half sick.

And so the waiting went on – each day a torture to be got through and over with. At the beginning, when I would wake up in my tiny cell, if the rays of the early morning sun could be seen latticed through the blinds I was content. The day had started right and the "coffee" would be strong and the marmalade not ration-card type. But now I awoke with a headache after a heavy, unsatisfying sleep and the first signs of life from Giuli gave me an active nausea at the thought of the responsibilities to come. All I wanted was to stay in bed until I was blasted out by a bomb or by the British and I thought one was quite as likely as the other – and both problematic. But there was an inner force that drove me ruthlessly and so I walked my miles around the garden and battled with the washing and the lessons and the disappointments on the days that Gemma had said she would come and I would spend vain hours haunting the gate, listening for the sound of a ring at the front door and footsteps in the corridor.

Between the cold and the damp and the scarce food we were both ripe for another bout of the flu. I put Giuli to bed and we stayed in our room swathed in a dirty red dressing gown which had stretched to uneven lengths and which, together with a series of hasty toilettes, made me look rather like the madam of a second-rate casino. I dragged around with running eyes and nose, deaf ears and a headache. I became a slattern in a red wool wrapper and I screamed and yelled and spanked and cursed. Our room was named San Giovanni Berchmans (all the convent rooms were named after saints) but at this point I re-christened it Le Petit Enfer. I kept wishing that I were a Catholic so that I could feel that at least I would be immune from purgatory at some later date and although I realized that all of these discomforts could only be classified as *petits misères* I didn't even have the satisfaction of offering them as daily tokens to some sadistic deity. Since I was perforce confined I suffered the air raids with fatalism. The railroad yards a short distance down the via Nomentana were a constant target and the whomp whomp of the bombs made the windows rattle and the room shake and the air itself seemed to vibrate. Until Giuli could be moved I fought down the instinct to run like a rabbit in any direction. I rubbed oil in my hair instead of washing it, as all hot water had to be lugged upstairs by Sœur Marie. Every week she would bring us hot water to bathe in and I would shut Giuli in the bathroom with me, give her a quick soaping and rinse and then spend half an hour wondering if I dared take my own clothes off and risk being caught by the sirens. Usually I climbed out and settled for a dab here and there without undressing completely.

I think I reached my all-time low the day the children got worms. Our little community of refugees had swelled – there were two women with numerous children, wives of Italian officers whom I suspected of being hidden in the gardener's cottage. From time to time I would catch a glimpse of Air-Force blue furtively slipping through the ilex trees in the garden. Then of course there was

Nadine. Nadine was a titled lady with a sharp wit and a languid manner who had gone into hiding, I suspected, because she thought it was the chic thing to do. When she tired of it after a few weeks she simply disappeared. But in the meantime I enjoyed her company immensely. She was plentifully supplied with goodies – heavenly treats like chocolate and cognac. Giuli ate the chocolates and I drank the cognac. I would go to Nadine's room at night and we would talk and sip and for a while I would be back in my own apartment in the via Panama entertaining guests, exchanging witticisms, patronizing the poor idiots who fell for the Fascist propaganda. Things again assumed their proper perspective and although the war was still there, for a while it was pushed into the background. I missed her sorely when she left and felt twice as lonely.

But to go back to the children. There were so many of them and they were all so dirty and whiny and thin and scared. There was just no more patience left to cope with them. It had rained and rained all through November and the garden was a soggy mess. Upstairs on the top floor where the children lived was the sour smell of diapers and unemptied potties and the younger ones scrubbed around underfoot, their little bare behinds sticking pertly up from underneath the thin shift, which was the only garment they wore. And so there I was walking around and around in the garden thinking of all those smelly wormy children upstairs and feeling very sorry for myself. Like a caged wild beast I plunged along the gravel path seeking to recapture my equilibrium – realizing I had to climb back onto a plane of philosophic acceptance of my situation or I couldn't go on. This had happened before and each time the climb back was more difficult, but I knew there was no alternative. If I allowed myself to fall too deeply into the chasm of despair and frustration I would feel physically ill and that frightened me. It was then, against strict orders and my better judgment, that I decided to ask one of the nuns to try to contact Gemma. Gemma was my dearest friend – the one person in all the world I truly loved. For six years we had been inseparable – mornings we talked on the phone, afternoons we spent prowling the city or sitting at home talking politics and in the evenings our husbands would join us and we would go out for dinner together. She had seen me through illnesses and love affairs and watched the gradual break-up of my marriage. Her home had sheltered me during the periodic separations from my husband and her practical Italian sense of intrigue combined with compromise had enabled me to keep going with some sense of composure. She was my mainstay, my councilor and my safety valve, and my present existence had become intolerable without the stimulation and solace that I found in her company. She supplied the optimism and vitality, which I lacked in my own character. I worked very carefully on the note I planned to smuggle out to her. I knew that her home had been searched during the hunt for Giulia and myself and I knew I could never forgive myself if any harm should come to her through me. I told her where I was and implored her to come and see me, but to be sure not to neglect to take all possible precautions. A week later she came – a bottle of wine in one hand! We embraced and looked at each other and laughed and cried and both talked at once. She bubbled over with news of the outside world – she was working with the underground. Her husband had gone into hiding so she had returned to live with her father and five sisters. They were hiding arms for the partisans. Her father was upset and apprehensive but to Gemma it was a game of wits with the authorities. She strutted around the room imitating the guttural German sounds and laughing at the gullibility of the Republican Fascists, as they now called themselves. They were being used to keep order and enforce the edicts laid down by the German authorities, but while the Germans had issued arms to them they didn't trust them enough to provide ammunition! This tickled the Roman sense of humor and the Blackshirts were victims of a good deal of heckling and practical jokes. I was starved for news of mutual friends, but some of the details of the social and moral disintegration that was taking place sounded weird and fantastic. Many of our friends were in hiding as I was, many had gone through the lines into Allied-occupied territory, many, especially the men, in the hope of a swift liberation, had gone to hospitals for minor operations such as appendicitis. A few had even entered the Forlanini Tuberculosis Sanitarium in order to present their release cards to the Germans. This was a most valuable document as the Germans had an inordinate fear of infection and as a rule would give the bearer a wide berth.

She also gave me a rundown on what had happened to Mario. I remembered him from another life – tall, good-looking, full of fun, and when he announced he was about to become a priest we didn't believe it. But he entered the novitiate and for a year and a half we saw no more of him. Then war broke out in September 1939 and the lights were lowered. Mario reappeared. He hadn't taken his final vows so he became a paratrooper. By that time Italy had a token number of troops in

France and one day Mario received a frantic letter from a friend of his serving there. The friend's fiancée, a Yugoslav, was about to be deported. Would Mario marry her to keep her in Italy until the friend could return? Mario certainly would and could. It was a fun wedding. After that I lost sight of him until Gemma showed up with news. By the winter of '43 he had become something of a legend among escaped prisoners of war hiding in the Abruzzi hills. He was from Bari, which had been occupied by the British 8th Army on its way up the east coast of the Italian peninsula. After a few days, carried away by a zealous desire to show some appreciation to the liberators, Mario presented himself at headquarters and announced that he was ready and willing to serve in any capacity. He knew the country, particularly that part of the Abruzzi Mountain, which was then borderline territory and seething with seditious country folk enraged against both Germans and Fascists alike.

He was received by a phlegmatic British major and taken at his voluble Italian word. He was instructed to pass through the lines into German-occupied Italy and from there to guide Allied soldiers, Italian civilians and whoever else was desirous of coming over to the Allied side. He was given a small compass to guide him and solemnly enjoined on pain of death to swallow it if he was ever in the least danger of capture. All of this was a bit more than he had bargained for, but he was determined to have a stab at it and not to fall down on his first assignment. I might add that material gain was very little incentive as the guides were given a thirty dollar bonus for officers, less for soldiers, and nothing for civilians.

He set off on foot clutching the dangerous compass

and when night came he was fairly far into German territory, so he found a cave in the rocks and holed up. The next morning he ran to the cave entrance and peered out upon a changed landscape. A white glittering carpet covered everything, the air was biting chill, and across the snowfield from the shelter of the neighboring woods advanced a German patrol. There was no escape so Mario closed his eyes and gulped down the compass and gave himself up.

He was taken for interrogation to a little town near Rieti. After being stripped and searched he was shoved naked into a cell from which he was taken twice daily for questioning. It was always the same. "You are a spy for the British, aren't you?" "Where did you come from?" "What are your instructions?" "Who is your commanding officer?" Then back to the cell again – naked, cold and hungry. But Mario had only one preoccupation. Where was the compass? Since the morning he had swallowed it, there had been no sign. Could it have been absorbed? Was it lying in wait, preparing for a fatal malady? Were compasses poisonous?

After a while, Mario was still worried, but the Germans were apparently satisfied. It was decided to evacuate him with a load of civilians headed north, forcible victims of the German fear of leaving potential sympathizers near the front, and so one morning a large group was piled onto an army truck tightly covered with canvas and launched onto the road heading towards Rimini. Mario was desperate. He had not kept faith with the signor maggiore, and then, the compass? He waited for his chance until the camion was well under way and then slit the tarpaulin with the pocketknife of one of his fellow travelers and eased himself through. He hit the dirt and lay on his face, not daring to move until the noise of the motor faded away down the bumpy twisting mountain road. When he ventured to lift his head turtlewise, he found that about fifteen others had followed his example and the road was dotted with prone figures cautiously inching their way toward the ditch. That was the last straw. He scrambled to his feet and started to run and before he realized it – and with no trouble at all – he was back in the British lines. He gasped out his story and demanded to be taken to Bari to his maggiore. The compass was still uppermost in his mind although en route he also began to feel very sheepish about turning up alone. No Allied officers, no ex-prisoners of war, not even a civilian to show for his excursion.

He arrived in Bari and haltingly explained his predicament. The signor maggiore listened kindly, but after a second look at Mario recommended, in fact ordered, a bath before continuing the colloquy. Mario was led away. An hour passed, two hours, and the major began to get impatient. So he set out to find this Eyetie who was perhaps double-crossing him. He opened the bathroom door and there was Mario squatting in a tub of water, a large hammer clutched in his hand and resignation and terror registered in every feature.

"What in hell are you doing with that?" asked the major crossly.

"Ai-ee Signor Maggiore!" wailed Mario pitifully. "Suppose I should feel ill with all that water around me? Suppose I should start to drown? I will give this tub one sharp tap with the hammer and ecco, all the water will run out. I do not want to be drowned, although with the compass inside of me I am liable to die anyway. Besides the sea is the place for swimming. I have never before swam inside of a house."

This may sound strange to Americans who probably don't know that in Italy in the thirties, and particularly in the south, there was no running water, no tubs and no showers. Water was filled into flasks from fountains in the village squares.

The compass, the compass. Mario was examined and X-rayed and pumped out and purged, but no trace of it was ever found and until the day he was killed he believed that he carried it about inside of him.

All of this took place in November. The major, being a good type and having little to lose, agreed to give Mario a second chance in his new career and by January, Mario had piled up a long list of escapees to his credit. He worked exclusively around the small Abruzzi hill towns where the scattered farms made policing difficult and almost every peasant had his protégé concealed in the house, barn or woods. Disgusted and fed up with the fascists, and loathing the Germans with true Italian nonchalance, these peasants risked their lives for no other reason than their hatred for the brutal tedeschi. Many of them became extremely fond of their dangerous guests and treated them as members of the family.

Christmas was drawing near and the sentimental implications of that season made life harder to bear. I was not always whining – in fact very little of the time. I forced myself to think no further ahead than the next hour and never to look back. I borrowed all the books the nuns were willing to lend me and consequently improved my French and learned more about the lives of more saints that I had ever known existed! Just before Christmas, a Jewish lady and her daughter were admitted to the convent. At first I was leery of making myself visible but after frequent overtures we became friendly, although I still could not reveal my identity. I used to take my knitting into their room at night after dinner and they insisted that I cheered them up. God knows I couldn't do it for myself. I had asked Gemma to see if she couldn't try to bring me something to make a Christmas tree and some inexpensive trinkets for Giulia's stocking. Our cell was so small that I had to stand a tiny branch on the prie-dieu, but it looked very festive. That night I wrote in my diary, "It is Christmas Eve." Christmas Eve! I cannot bear to think of it. What a Christmas. I suppose everybody tonight will think as I do... will recall other Christmases, happier times, let themselves go in an orgy of self-pity. It is laughable, my pathetic attempts to create a Christmas spirit for Giulia. I do want her to feel as I do about it and that can only happen if I teach her those emotions of childhood which are so precious and even though they now cause me so much pain, I wouldn't be without it. I try so hard, but it is uphill work. I feel enthusiastic about the tree and the stocking. I have composed a lovely crèche in our room but Giuli doesn't participate. It is ridiculous that a child of five should be able to smother enthusiasm the way she can. This evening we came upstairs and I asked her, "Now, what do we do before going to bed?" Naturally I expected her to say, "Hang up the stockings," as I had carefully coached her about Santa Claus and the Christmas tree, but instead, with the resigned tone of a prospective flu victim she said, "Put in the nose drops." I felt failure cropping out on me like a rash! I went to three consecutive Christmas masses, which lasted until three in the morning and although I didn't understand much of the ritual I was slightly comforted. On returning to my room I glued myself as usual to my little green radio tuned to the BBC. I tuned in to *Forces Favorites* and it was playing Bing Crosby's *I'll Be Home for Christmas* and for the first time I felt complete despair and started to cry. What was it that Noel Coward had written about "the potent power of cheap music"? "Home seemed a magic word...", "The black fox has left his hole", "Water over the dam", "Red is next to black"; what did they mean and who were they meant for? I had great admiration and a slight touch of envy for Jean and her girlfriend. They appeared to be so unconcerned and fearless. One night Jean came on the air and announced, "Gillian should be along any moment – she got bombed out last night and has spent the day looking for new digs!" What a typical example of gallant nonchalance and how I wished I could be more like that. One evening when I was feeling particularly lonely and depressed I heard a very British voice coming over the airwaves talking about – of all things – trains! I listened and pretty soon I started to laugh and before long I was convulsed and wiping away tears of hysterical mirth. It was a record of Reginald Gardner's called *Trains*. Years later I met Mr. Gardner and was able to thank him for saving my life and my sanity one cold winter evening in the middle of the war. The broadcasts always ended with four musical notes – da da da dum. I didn't know what that signified either. In a sense I wasn't strictly alone on those quiet – except for the clock – evenings. There were always the planes. Until the bombing really got started there would only be one or two. It would drone overhead and then there would be three or four explosions and then I knew it was safe to go to bed. In spite of the newspaper headlines screaming

"Allied Atrocities" everyone knew it was either a German or Fascist plane and its target was always a hospital or convent. A maternity clinic close to us was bombed and I learned later that Dr. Rubiani, my gynecologist, had been killed. A few days after we entered the convent the Vatican was bombed. Four bombs were dropped and the damage was considerable. This caused a terrific stir among the nuns and although they were wary of committing themselves they knew that it was not the British. Most of the nuns were French except for Mother Perry and Mother Hermans, while the sisters were all Italian. These lone planes always left a residue of booby-trapped objects in their wake, exploding fountain pens to be picked up by children, many of whom were blinded or had an arm or a hand blown off. Giuli had strict orders *never* to touch anything she might find lying on the ground.

Christmas. I tried not to remember other Christmases. Waking as a child early on a grey morning and tingling with excitement at the sight of a lumpy outline at the foot of the bed. The candlelight service at St. James church with all the familiar carols and afterwards coming out into the cold and seeing Park Avenue sparkling with Christmas trees. The traditional family dinner with all the elderly relatives passing out crisp new dollar bills and all of us children sitting together for the turkey dinner with the softly polished silver and shining crystal and the furtive thrill of drinking real cider! Giuli had no part in these memories for me and that is why I labored to create some for us together.

I composed a lovely crèche and told Christmas stories and explained about the tree and the stocking and the presents, but she was apathetic and listless and so my enthusiasm trailed off into bitter thoughts and negative feelings and the all-too-familiar hopelessness and despair. Christmas Eve, from my diary: I cannot bear to think of it, I suppose everybody tonight will think as I do, will recall other Christmases, happier times, let themselves go in an orgy of self pity. This is the season of good will, but I feel no will, neither good nor will. Motherhood is drudgery and I have nothing to cling to, no love, no hope, mean thoughts with which to while away the time waiting for midnight mass. We have a midnight service in our church too. New York; it is cold tonight and Fifth Avenue is lit at intervals with Christmas trees. The family is probably dining all together and there is a big tree and the uncles and the cousins and the aunts are exchanging news. Do they remember me after six years? Do they wonder where I am tonight and if I am alive or dead? They don't know how close I am to them in spirit. Oh, much more then to anyone who is near me now. Giulia sleeps in her bed and I look at her. Who is she? Tonight I don't know her. She has no memories for me. And then I thought – one day all this will only be memory. Perhaps, in later years, I shall recall my stay here in the convent mellowed and softened by time like a pastel, with gratitude and humility. I will remember the goodness of the nuns, the evenings I spent with Ninon chatting over a thimbleful of vile Italian cognac, the pathetic little tree and presepio that I made for Giuli, and I will smile and forget the long lonely evenings, the lousy days of rain when Giuli was irritable and I was at my wit's end, the sacrifice of flesh and spirit that it seems to me now.

And then something happened to shock me out of my self-indulgent self-pity. I was struggling with my knitting in the Rossi's room and the Jewish lady, her daughter and sister were trying to show me how to add a stitch without leaving a hole! They had saved me a bit of dried fruit and we were chatting about the rumors of increased activity against the religious houses by the Republican Fascists. Ever since the November bombing of the Vatican, the Germans had been inclined to be rather conciliatory, but the Fascists had no scruples about invading pontifical property. In fact, they had become so infuriated at the Vatican for not recognizing their absurd Republic that they had started breaking into convents, churches and monasteries all over Rome.

It was almost midnight when Sœurmarie knocked on the door and told Signora Rossi that there was a Jesuit priest downstairs asking to speak with her. I accompanied the three of them down to the reception hall where a bearded father was waiting. Gently he told them that the Oriental Institute had been raided, that one of their men had managed to escape over the roofs, but that Signora Rossi's husband had suffered a heart attack from the shock and since Rosa's fiancé was a doctor he had refused to leave him. He couldn't tell us any more but promised to send someone the next day to let us know the outcome. We spent the rest of the night in the parlor in the dark and the cold and in the morning Father Ignazio returned to tell us that Signor Rossi was dead and the Fascists had taken Dr. Giacobbe away. The Signora's grief was wild, uncontrolled and primitive. All that day and night she sat in front of her husband's picture rocking to and fro and wailing.

"Ai, he was a good provider!

"Ai, he was a model husband!

"Ai! He was a noble father!

"Ai! The world has lost a virtuous and honorable

man!"

She railed against the fate that had taken him from them so prematurely, and she cursed the instruments of that fate, calling them excommunicates, murderers.

While all this was going on my husband came for a visit. I had nothing to say to him, no feeling to share. Perhaps I was too tired, perhaps it was because we had arrived at a point without mutual love, respect or even friendship. Perhaps I felt subconsciously that had he been at the Oriental Institute one of my problems would now be solved. It sounds dreadful now, but in those days everything was dreadful. It was the season of grief and not goodwill.

The day after Christmas the body of Signor Rossi was brought to the chapel and Father Ignazio returned for the funeral mass and to discuss arrangements for the burial. The Signora was worn out, stupefied, and to make matters worse, the Roman cemetery, Campo Verano, had suffered so severely in the first bombing of Rome back in July that few people were being allowed in. Graves had been ripped open and since then coffins had just been piling up at the entrance.

"Ai, what shall we do?" the Signora lamented. "I do not understand this tactic of bombing the already dead. Our plot in the Catholic cemetery has been bombed and now we have no place to lay our poor husband."

"We have a tomb in the Jewish cemetery for the unconverted members of the family," Rosa suggested. "Perhaps we could lay papa there until such time as our plot is in order and he can be moved."

Father Ignazio shook his head. "For that I will have to speak to the Father Superior," he said. The next day the Father Superior talked with the Signora. "I don't know," he said. "It is wartime and many unhallowed things are happening, but this, well, I will talk to the Bishop." The Bishop was doubtful about taking the responsibility, but he promised to intercede with the cardinal.

The cardinal was a wise and tolerant man. Since the beginning of the war there had been many deviations from protocol. Convents and monasteries overflowed with heretics, escaped prisoners and victims of persecution. The Vatican had opened its heart and its doors.

"Reverend Father," he said to the Superior of the Jesuits, "bury the poor man with my blessing. He is lucky to have a burial at all, unlike those who are fighting in our mountains. If 'they' ever get here, well, we shall see. In the meantime, in this season of His birthday, Our Lord, who was Himself of that faith, will not, I am sure begrudge anyone a temporary resting place…"

And so the dispensation was granted and the Signora Rossi had a happy new year after all. The next best thing to having her husband with her was the assurance that now, at least, he had a chance in the hereafter. Dr. Giacobbe was never heard from again.

By the middle of January, I had been in hiding for four months and I felt I had reached the end of my tether. The only words I spoke during the day were either to Giuli or to the nuns and when I went to my room at night the tears of loneliness rolled down my cheeks and in the quiet I could hear them dropping on my clothes and on the floor. All the false business into which I had forced myself – the knitting, the French and philosophy lessons, the reading and crossword puzzles – had required a determination and discipline which I was no longer able to maintain. All control had left me and a nervous agitation took over that made me feel as if I was going mad. I couldn't bear the sight of the nuns and during the day I would flee to the most hidden parts of the garden – in the evening I lurked in the corridor so I wouldn't have to stop and speak to them. Giuli affected me in the same way. Our meals together were agony, the quality of the food had deteriorated until our diet consisted mainly of coarse bread and a soup made out of a rough paste both of which I strongly suspected – and have since had confirmed – contained an ample sprinkling of sawdust. In the afternoons and evenings, I would chase her away from me and finally I decided I would risk sending her to school in the mornings accompanied by the elderly mother of the gardener. The first morning I hid in the bathroom to watch them setting forth together, the old woman and the little girl, a badly knitted white scarf wound around her neck, the two of them hand in hand walking out of the gate, and I cried and cried. I paced up and down the room crying, hating what I was doing to Giuli and hating what the war was doing to us both. I cried for God to help me as I no longer had the capacity to help myself and I kept repeating Bianchi's desperate cry, "God, if there be a God, save my soul, if I have a soul."

My one tie with reality was Gemma. I concentrated all of my positive feelings on her – I felt that outside of her friendship there was no other love, no other purpose to my life. I was jealous of the time she couldn't spend with me. I despised my husband and all the other men who I knew were hiding, armed and doing nothing to chase the Germans out of the city, but complaining bitterly about the slowness of the Allied advance. I knew Gemma had a link with the underground and so I asked her if she could talk to Mario about taking Giuli and myself through the lines on his next trip. I felt I had nothing to lose and anything was preferable to my present existence – a quick death while making the attempt to reach freedom was infinitely desirable compared to the slow day-by-day death, which I felt inside myself.

On January 13, the bombings started again in earnest. The planes roared overhead in formation heading for the airfields – it was a frightening sound as we knew that the farce of Rome being an "open" city was no secret, but there were rumors that the Allies had some kind of a precision bombsite and we kept telling ourselves that they could easily avoid hitting us. Then came the news of the Anzio landings! Finally! Finally, I thought we are nearing the end – I was half crazy thinking of our troops only fifty miles from Rome. Surely they couldn't bog down and waste another month before getting here. It was so cold, and the food was so short. I had acquired what I called a "siege silhouette" and the nervous strain of five or six alarms and bombings a day were taking a greater toll of my overwrought nerves. I felt that I had held out for so long that I simply couldn't afford to go to pieces now that the end seemed in sight. I looked on Giulia as more and more of a millstone around my neck – without her I would have been free to take my chance.

The Allied beach head at Anzio brought a breath of fresh air and bolstered the lagging spirits with its promise of imminent liberation, but the days dragged and no advance was made and in the meantime the air raids grew more frequent. We had learned that the alarms were not usually reliable but the doubt was there all the same. What was much worse was the solitary German or Fascist plane which would cruise above the city at night and drop three or four bombs on some clinic or convent so that the next day the headlines would scream, "New Allied atrocities!" A maternity hospital next door had been bombed and we wondered when our turn would come.

From my diary:

> February 15, 1944: The new Allied landing at Anzio bolstered up the old morale quite a bit and when a week afterward the distant roar of cannon, like surf on a nearby beach, began to be heard day and night, I thought perhaps the time had come to permit my thoughts to wander into the future. But no, the old snail campaign is still going on, add to that the nervous strain of continuous bombardments and fresh persecution of Giulia and myself. It has gotten to the point now where I cannot hear an airplane without flinching and ducking my head – as if that would do any good! The English bomb us in the daytime and the Germans at night – naturally attributing it to the former. So far they have hit two hospitals and I expect them at any moment to pass to the convents. So sure am I of not getting out of this situation alive that I feel that I should have acquired some resignation or at least a facade of nonchalance – but alas!

Finally, I decided that I could no longer cope with Giulia's education so I arranged for the gardener's wife to take her to a kindergarten around the corner. I still never set foot outside and Gemma's infrequent visits were my only bright spots. In the garden I had paced off an area equal to 500 meters that looped and doubled back on itself to make a figure eight and I forced myself to walk the equivalent of five kilometers a day. One stretch brought me past the potato patch and I learned to measure their growth with a practiced eye as by now food was growing extremely scanty. The sister convent at Albano had been bombed out and the survivors had landed on us, bringing our total to eighty and the available food supply was hardly sufficient to nourish half that number. One day a peasant arrived with a cow, pleading to be allowed to hide it in our garden from the Germans and we were given our first taste of butter in many months. Both Giulia and I had stomach cramps for days, which made me realize the lack of fats we were suffering from. Then there was the pigsty! Two beautiful pigs were fattening for our consumption! I always lingered over the sty counting the ribs and loins and gathering acorns from the ilax trees. These pigs were to prove my undoing. One day as usual I was draped over the fence waiting for Gulia to come back from school. She had just come in the back gate when I heard the familiar hum of airplane motors in the distance. I looked up and saw several formations of American planes flying in our direction. The sky behind them was black with flack and bits of it were beginning to rain into the garden. I grabbed Giulia by the hand and started running toward the house. Suddenly, there was a terrific burst and we both were knocked flat and pieces of glass showered down all around us. Two bombs landed in the pigsty. We picked ourselves up and made for the house. Everything was in confusion, windowpanes still tinkling onto the staircase and smoke drifting all over us. I went to an open doorway under an arch and kneeling down took Giuli into my arms. She was terrified, sobbing and crying and embracing me with all of her might, her little face turned up as she cried over and over again, "*Gesu! non piu bomba!*

Gesu! vieni da me!" I was all too afraid we were going to Him and could only hug her tighter as the infernal symphony crashed down around us and I imagined that every second could blow us all into bits. The house shook as the planes seemed to hover above us and load after load of bombs exploded in the garden. I wanted to crawl into something, to burrow deep and hide. I felt naked and exposed. I couldn't feel my heart beat and I thought it must have stopped. I struggled to get my breath. My mouth was dry and there was a strange taste in it. Giulia's body was rigid in my arms as she screamed and screamed.

When the first wave had passed we shakily picked ourselves up to examine the damage, but in less than half an hour we heard another wave approaching. We ran to another doorway and knelt and the nuns started reciting the rosary. Giulia kept saying, "*Non voglio un'altra bomba! Gesu, non un'altra bomba!*" I felt like that too. Please God, not another bomb, not today, not now.

When it was over we went into the garden again. Our small potato patch was ruined, a close hit on the pigpen had scattered our carefully nurtured pork chops over a hundred square yards of lawn and all that was left of the spot on which I had been standing was a crater dug by a five hundred pound bomb. In all, eight bombs had fallen on the house and in the garden, three of which remained unexploded. The nuns called the local bomb-disposal squad but they refused to come. They just said not to get too close and after a week or so there wouldn't be any more danger. We didn't know any better and pretty soon thought no more about it even though one was directly in the path of my daily walk. We sent the gatekeeper out for news, to find out what had happened and how much damage had been done. The Tiburtina railroad station was at the end of our street, via Nomentana, and the full length had been bombed. Overhearing this I lost my head completely. Gemma lived at the far end of the via. I had to find out if she was all right. I didn't dare phone from the convent. For the first time in four months I stepped outside the walls. The devastation was frightening. Frantically, I started to run up the street looking for a house intact enough to have a telephone. Finally, I came opposite a clinic. They were bringing the wounded in for treatment, even though the place itself had been badly damaged. People were lying all over the floor, bleeding on the broken glass from the windows and squads of men were digging through the wreckage. I didn't pay any attention to any of it. I just noticed in a hazy way what was going on. Reaching a telephone was the only thought in my mind. No one paid any attention to me as I tore through the place. There it was and with only a slight delay I managed to get through. Gemma was all right. Hearing her voice on the phone I burst into tears – she had been just about to start out to come looking for me. She and her family were evacuating that afternoon to Piazza Navona, right in the heart of Rome. It was miles away from me and I wouldn't see her again. But she would be safe. She implored me not to take any chances of being picked up, but to get right back to the convent. I would have liked to prolong my taste of freedom. I wasn't really afraid of the Germans – a feeling based purely on ignorance, not courage – but I hated them too much to fear them. When I saw them or heard them talking, the intensity of my hatred obliterated any other feeling.

From that day on life became pure and simple hell.

Waves of nervous agitation would awake me at four in the morning and I would spend the day poised to run for cover. Every siren, every distant buzz even if it turned out to be only a bumble bee sent my heart somersaulting and my blood alternately hot and cold, and in the evening, crying spells left me exhausted. I had learned to tell the different types of planes by their sound. Of course the Stukas were the easiest and we had been hearing them for a long time but now with the Americans coming in the daytime and the English at night, plus the occasional lone German night bomber, my ears became attuned. I crouched over my little radio in the evenings, straining to hear the BBC to find out what was happening to us. So I learned the names of the planes: Lancaster, Liberators, Spitfires, Flying Fortresses. Hundreds of them roared back and forth over our heads night after night, but in the dark it wasn't as frightening. There was nothing to be done and nowhere to go so I listened to each wave as it passed over and tried to get some sleep during the lulls. I didn't feel safe and I didn't want to die and Giulia was driving me crazy in her own way. Her defenses were as strong as mine, and to me she seemed impertinent, disobedient and completely self-centered. I tried to get through to her, but the wall was too thick and we each had to live on our own side and suffer in our own way. My inability to love her under those conditions was countered by her stubborn resistance to acknowledge any emotion not directly connected with herself. Thank God she had Mother Hermans, the young, beautiful Belgian nun, of whom she was very fond and who perhaps took the place in her life that Gemma did in mine.

March 11 was Giulia's sixth birthday. My husband

came to spend the afternoon with her and I took him into the garden to see the damage. He told me I was an ass to be afraid and that the air raids weren't worth worrying about. He was safe in Vatican City! The nuns had prepared a birthday surprise for Giuli, a little cupcake, and so we went into the house earlier than usual. I was allowed to take my husband upstairs to show him our new room, our former quarters having been destroyed by a bomb. We were leaning out of the window looking into the garden when one of the unexploded bombs went off, the one I had been sitting on earlier. Stones and shell fragments rattled down on the roof and all I could think of was how lucky we were to have been called in for tea half an hour early.

We were now without water, gas and electricity, but since things like washing had long since passed into the limbo of dimly remembered activities of another life, it didn't really matter. I got thinner and my complexion took on a greenish tinge and there was a continual ringing in my ears. The days were getting longer and I suffered intensely from the cold. I hadn't seen or heard from Gemma since the bombing and I was growing concerned, until one day, towards the end of the month, a letter was dropped off at the gatehouse telling me she had been ill. "Don't worry about my being careful," she wrote. "I shall be more than that so as to get well and be able to come to you, whom I think about night and day. Believe me when I say that I will grasp at any opportunity to let you know how great is the affection that ties me to you and how sure I am that all through our lives we shall be friends in the most sincere and profound sense of the word. Together we have shared joys, sorrows, pain, and I feel as if we had been together for ever and I cannot imagine a life without you." I felt the same way and this cherished letter took precedence over everything – even the extraordinary rumor that the Germans were leaving Rome. I couldn't believe it. It seemed too good to be true. The Allies were bogged down at Cassino – why would the Germans want to leave? The phony story, I learned, was to stop the air raids, but since they still talked about Rome being an "open" city nobody knew what to believe. Everyone was suspicious and discontented and restless and "incidents" occurred with increasing frequency.

Then came the affair of the via Rasella and horror shrouded the city as bit by bit the details rode to the surface. A group of partisans posing as street sweepers had hidden a bomb in a dustman's cart and set it off just as a German patrol was coming up the hill of the little street. Twenty-six Germans were killed and twenty wounded. Reprisals were immediately instituted and hostages were taken and hauled off to the Gestapo torture chambers in via Tasso. This was standard procedure and the usual proportion was ten Italians for every one German killed. It was from Gemma that I finally learned more details of what she referred to as "the Ardeatine caves massacre". One of her partisan friends had gone afterwards to see if he could recover some of the bodies, but they had been covered with pitch and were all stuck together. It was said that more than five hundred were rounded up and hauled out to the catacombs where they were shot and dumped into one of the caves. Years later, when Robert Katz wrote a book *Death in Rome* about this tragedy, including a list of names of those massacred, I checked off four friends of mine among those killed. Unfortunately, Mr. Katz had an irrational bias against the

Vatican and claimed that the Pope knew of the coming reprisal. The Vatican sued and won the case against this claim, since everyone knew what would happen. The city walls were plastered with posters announcing that the Germans would exact ten for one if a German was shot. The two "partisans" responsible were Carla Capponi and her lover, General Bentivegna, both Communists. If they had come forward and admitted their part the Ardeatine caves massacre would have been avoided, but no, Communists are cowards and the party line does not contemplate admitting atrocities. Contrast this with the story of a young Carabiniere in a small town north of Rome, Salvo Dacquisto, who came forward after some Germans were killed, claimed responsibility, and was promptly shot. Carla Capponi and her General friend were elected later to the Italian parliament.

All of a sudden, it was Easter and as April advanced, the glories of the Roman spring slowly unfolded. My memories turned nostalgically to other springs – that time of the year when one is alternatively restless and lethargic, filled with vitality and dreamy at the same time. It was the time when I would come home with my arms filled with the deep pink sprays of flowering peach, the first sweet sign of the season. Judas trees with their purple and magenta fantasy burst into flower in the green haven of the Villa Borghese and white oleanders lined the sidewalk of the via Veneto. At the foot of the Trinita dei Monti the flower vendors set up their stalls and all of a sudden Piazza di Spagna was carpeted, with spring surrounding Bernini's fountain lovingly called the barcaccia. The little rowing clubs swinging beside the yellow Tiber vibrated with life and the receding water left their gardens lush and verdant. On Sundays, we would drive out into the country, to the lakes or up to the Castelli to sample the new wine, and in the evening when the cool breeze swept up from Ostia, nightingales called to each other from the umbrella pines in the garden across the street from my bedroom. The days were hot and long and lazy and twilight came early with its damp mist curling from the river. In the convent garden wisteria and snapdragon bordered the path of my daily walk. I decided to put my restlessness to use. I would make soap.

I enlisted the aid of Antonia, the gardener's mother. She knew all about it and by devious means procured the necessary ingredients. It seemed to need a great deal of animal fat scraps, caustic soda, and I don't remember what else. We lugged a huge cauldron out by the bombed-out potato patch and took turns stirring and ladling. In the afternoons I would sit in the sun on an unexploded bomb while Giuli played around with bits and pieces of broken glass and for a brief period of time I was almost happy. The sun was warm and my blood was starting to circulate. The bombings were more at night now than in the daytime. Occasionally, Giuli would dig up a potato and there were a couple of artichoke plants that didn't seem to be doing anything but looking pretty in their fuzzy fashion. Our soap smelled horrible. We stirred and stirred and the fumes were choking. This went on for three days as the fire was small and it was hard to keep it going. But gradually, the mixture thickened and was ready to pour into molds. We used Antonia's kitchen utensils and carefully ladled it out to let it settle and harden and finally there it was. Coarse and yellow and smelly and of an undetermined consistency, but unquestionably soap!

Sister Teresa had a little balcony overlooking the garden and I would sit there in the brief period between benediction and supper and look at the familiar scene from a new perspective, transformed by the evening sky. The stridency of the martins overhead almost drowned out the sound of buses on the via Nomentana. A distant bombardment – or were "they" close enough for it to be cannon? – provided a bass undertone. A little pool reflected the small bordering trees, the lopsided pine, so irritating to the symmetry, leaned blandly over the chicken run, that peculiar Italian brand of oak or ilex blotted out the view of the left hand corner and the chirrup of the nuns at recreation rivaled the twitter of the nesting birds. They did not need to seek the evening to find peace.

Spring came and went as April passed into May and, as the earth settled down to a grim summer aridity, my spiritual life shriveled until I felt like the driest of parched earth. I could not swallow Catholic doctrine, but I prayed for belief in even a Protestant god and over and over I repeated Bianchi's despairing cry. I grew sick to death of my thoughts. I was sick of thinking about God and trying to connect Him with the beliefs and doctrines with which I was in daily contact. I was sick of the perpetual spiritual struggles; sick of the present and unconvinced that there would be a future. As always I drew on the past for comfort. Ever since I could remember I had done this. Nothing seemed too bad once it was over and if I did not allow myself to be happy in the present, in the past there was always safety. And so I tried to project the present and make it the past. Some day, I thought, I will look back with nostalgia on this evening scene. My love and nostalgia for Rome itself was already a part of my life, too many memories, too many affections were bound up for this not to be so, but the present was a period apart. It was not linked with anything or anyone. It was a period of trials, of patience, endurance and solitude. At times in my musings and meandering through the past, I would dredge up the sins I had committed and feel that I was being punished for them, and at other times I would feel that God must have a special "tendresse" for me because He was driving me mad.

With the fall of Cassino on May 20, I picked my spiritual chin up off the floor and whirled into a burst of mechanical activity to keep myself from thinking. Mother Hermans procured for me a typewriter and I forced myself to practice two hours a day. I translated Shakespeare sonnets into Italian, I wrote pages of poetry, I started my autobiography (in Italian) but upon reaching the age of twelve, I found it so depressing I gave up! The offensive against the Gustav line had begun. The cannons rumbled and seemed to be coming nearer. We hoped and prayed for anything – starvation, epidemics, bombardments – anything to see the end. I could no longer go to church – I wanted to live, and I felt I was being buried alive. Everyone wondered what the Germans would do when they had to leave. Explosions and artillery fire ringed the city day and night. Some said the Germans were blowing up the bridges and airfields, some said they would destroy the water supply; eventually they blew the hydro-electric plants at Tivoli leaving us for over a year without power. The weather grew hotter and as the Allied advance continued I felt I could not keep inside my skin with the nervous agitation. To be free! To breathe free air, to be at peace among my own kind. To say, "This is mine," and feel it to be so. Not to support any longer this nausea of things, persons, ideas. Not to hate – or to be hated and persecuted. I didn't hate, I despised. "Tomorrow and tomorrow" and perhaps now tomorrow had really come. Our troops were in the Alban hills. At night we would go up on the roof to watch the red flashes from the guns. For three days we neither ate nor slept – bombs to the right of us, cannon to the left of us, dive-bombers overhead and only God knew who or what around us. Every day the danger of discovery and death grew greater but this time there was real hope of relief. The night of June 2 was fantastic! Voices in the street and contradicting rumors buzzed relentlessly. The Americans were arriving – they were at Porta Pia; unable to bear it I ran out, outside the wall in my bedroom slippers and for a moment felt bewildered. A prisoner who has finished a jail sentence must feel the same way when he first sets foot in the street and feels people all about him, and life, and motion. I had scarcely gone three paces when a land mine blew up. I ducked back to the shelter of the gate. A few moments passed and I decided to try it again – but with the same results. The house across the street had been a Fascist militia head-quarters and I imagined that the entire place had been honeycombed with mines. All of a sudden life seemed too precious. It was life again, not existence and vegetation and, much as it cost me not to go out and drink in the spectacle of American troops entering Rome, I decided to be prudent. There were some people standing in the garden and I went to ask if it were true; if the troops we could see going up the street were American or German. At night it was hard to tell as the helmets were so alike. One man offered to go out and we waited breathlessly for his return. He came back drooping. "Well?" we enquired.

"No, Signora," he said sadly. "They are still the retreating Germans."

"But are you sure?" I asked. "How do you know?"

"I went up to one of them, signora," he replied, "and I asked him, 'Are you American?' and he said to me 'Yah'!"

"They are! They are! They are!" I cried. I knew at last we were in!

Monday, June 5, 1944. The troops came in at two in the morning. All night long cannon had flared on the neighboring hills and the retreating enemy had skirmishes in the suburbs and mines were detonated under bridges, in the gardens and their bordering villas. By five in the morning the city was "liberated" and the populace had begun timidly to creep from hiding. At eight in the morning, my husband and mother-in-law appeared at the convent. Her reunion with Giuli was emotional and touching and I left the two of them embracing each other with the understanding that Giuli would stay with her grandmother until my own vague future could be worked out. I told my husband coldly that I was going to get a legal separation and that I would be in touch with him. For the first time in nine years of marriage I was able to look him in the eye without fear of reprisal and say what was in my heart. More than Rome was liberated that day.

The convent's iron gate clicked open for me and I emerged into the blinding Italian sunlight of that June morning. The streets looked unfamiliar. A wave of joy surged through me as I gazed around incredulously. Free again! Finished, the nightmare of bombings and searchings, shooting in the alleys after curfew and the daily problem of food. The streets were swarming with people on foot except for the strange little military vehicles with their four-man crews. Great tanks rolled down the via Nomentana with grinning, dusty, red-eyed soldiers sprawled over the turrets festooned with flowers. Young girls raced alongside waving Italian and American flags, and at every halt clambered aboard to embrace the soldiers while the cheering onlookers risked a messy death underneath the treads in their efforts to get a better view. Gigantic guns towed by small tractors snaked their way along the tram-car lines. The men waved bottles of wine and cheered. One group had obviously had time for a bit of souvenir hunting during one of the halts. The driver was decorated with a fine bit of ancient armor. An antique breastplate rose above the dashboard. His companion waved a halberd and another sported a medieval helmet complete with plumes. A steady roar hummed over the whole city as the serpentine column wound its intricate way through the streets. Not a moment's hesitation from the time it entered the main gate, rounded the cemetery, streaked down the widest thoroughfare with thunderous speed to weave its way past the gardens down to the river. Then out the north gate and over the Ponte Milvio with unflagging pace, less than a kilometer behind the last German stragglers.

It was pandemonium – hysteria – liberation. It was army trucks already distributing loaves of white bread in the streets; it was dog-tired infantrymen being waylaid with the everlasting cry "Sigarette!" It was the last chapter in the book of occupation with all of its accompanying terrorism and weary expectancy agonizingly prolonged.

Breathlessly I started to walk heading for the Piazza Navona and Gemma. The American voices sounded strange in the familiar surroundings. Strange and beautiful. Exaltation and excitement mounted to an almost hysterical pitch as I fought my way through the throngs. I waltzed the length of the Nomentana to Porta Pia, with its statue of Bersagliere, the site of the famous "breccia", when the King's troops liberated Rome from the Vatican. Down the via Venti Settembre and then Piazza Barberini, with its beautiful trident fountain, to the main post office and from there threading my way through cobblestoned streets almost to the river. Things were quieter down by the river. People still gave the bridges a wide detour for fear of mines, but for once I felt no fear. The tall Texan guards meant security; the little stubby-winged planes circling overhead were watchful eagles – American Eagles.

Finally I reached Piazza Navona, where Gemma had been evacuated. The most beautiful piazza in the world, with its gorgeous fountains. I love most the rivers fountain – the Nile, the Ganges, the Danube and finally the South American Plate holding up its hand in horror towards the façade of the Borromini church, Bernini's way of telling his rival that he feared the church would fall on him! My heart was beating in my throat and my breath was coming in short gasps and the top of my head felt as if it were floating about three inches above my ears. I had walked over twelve miles without any food, no rest for several days and in a state of euphoria balanced delicately on the edge of sanity. I barely made it up the wide marble staircase leading to Gemma's apartment in the Palazzo Lancellotti – almost next door to the infamous Palazzo Braschi where the Republican Fascists had had their torture chambers and prison. Weak, panting, sore-footed and ecstatic, I fell into Gemma's arms, the five sisters scurried about for water for me to wash, for wine for me to drink and Papa bellowed for someone to bring food.

There could be no more appropriate time than right now for me to institute a parenthesis and describe Gemma's family while I am catching my breath from my long walk across Rome. Anna was the eldest, the *distinta* as the Italians say. Fastidious, peremptory, level-headed, discreet and with a will of iron. Adelina came next. Adelina was the gay one, the live-today-for-tomorrow-we-die one, as indeed she was to do before very long. Life was to be lived and no physical disability or moral persuasion would cause her to deviate. She was gallant and reckless and the only person she ever hurt was herself. She had to die young and in a way I am glad for her that she did. Vittoria was the staid one. She had her own life, engaged to an Italian youth and while engagements and marriages were breaking up all around her under the onslaught and blandishments of the Allied Occupation troops, Vittoria took no part in any of it and continued to go to bed – alone, with her fiancé's picture under her pillow. Gemma, my alter ego, was a curious mixture. She had adored her mother and upon her death some years ago had suffered a breakdown. She had a quick mind and could out-talk and out-reason the glibbest politician, philosopher, lawyer, or whoever dared to cross verbal swords with her. She had a passionate nature – passionate in her loves and in her hates – but it was tempered by that curious Italian instinct for seeing the reality of things and situations that so often escape the Anglo-Saxon mind and so continues to promote the myth of the emotionally uncontrollable Latin. Nanda and Gabriella were younger, stayed pretty much to themselves and were known as *le sorelline* the little sisters. Then of course, and I mean no disrespect by leaving him until last, since after all his was the responsibility, there was Papa. Papa was known to everyone as Il Commendatore. He made his living in some mysterious way that involved deals with various ministries, telephone calls to senators, the expediting of matters for clients – not that there was anything shady. I suppose one could call him a one-man lobby. He knew which palm to grease and whose back needed scratching. His bark was loud and threatening, his bite wouldn't have disturbed the whipped cream topping on a cake and there wasn't one of us that couldn't wind him around our little finger. Particularly Adelina. There were certain traits that were shared by the whole family, after all they were Calabrese, among which were generosity and warm-heartedness. And so it was into this nest of love and laughter and total acceptance that I floundered like a tired homing pigeon.

The Piazza Navona had been taken over by an advance group, which had come in the night before and already work was progressing under the blazing sun. We all leaned out of the apartment windows and watched the soldiers bustling about. My first instinct was to dash down and join up, but I wasn't quite sure how to go about it. Years of being almost a hostage in an alien and hostile country had sharpened my patriotism to a hysterical pitch. I knew I could be useful as I had lived in Italy off and on since I was fifteen – for the last seven years continuously – and spoke the language like a native. In fact, neither my husband nor my daughter spoke any English. I was well informed on the political set-up and I knew who was who and – more important – who was where. Between myself and the Fazzari family, I also knew where a lot of the bodies were buried. I felt that I had so much to make up as my heretofore attempts at flag waving had only served to get me into trouble. All that was behind me. I was once more the proud citizen of the greatest country in the world and free to proclaim it in public and in private before whomever I pleased. I also felt that I had a duty to support my many friends and acquaintances who through the year had sacrificed much to avoid joining with the Fascists – newspaper men who had become jobless for refusing to follow the propaganda line, film directors who were refused financing for not making pictures glorifying the regime, businessmen who had had to live unobtrusively from hand to mouth trying to avoid the coils of the corporate state, politicians who had been interned or exiled for open defiance of Fascist policies – I was so sure that the Allies would want to know about these people that they would welcome them and reward them with respect and jobs. Not that any of these people were looking for rewards or even recognition – their one aim was eagerness to offer their services.

The Fazzaris, being a practical family, suggested that I go down to the square and speak to the commanding officer and ask if any of the men would like to come up for a wash. There wasn't any hot water but they were sure that soldiers wouldn't object to cold baths. I descended to the square. A canvas had been strung between two jeeps to protect the officers working at improvised desks. Groups of children clustered outside the barbed wire barricade, as yet too awestruck to start begging. I just stood there feeling too shy even to approach the guard. I knew they were my own people, but would they know that? I had been away from home for so long – even the language sounded strange. I had no documents, no proof of my identity. I forced myself to approach an M.P. and said in a shaky voice "Sir, I am an American. Is it possible to speak to your commanding officer?"

Commander Ronald Lena R.C.N.V.R. (Royal Canadian Navy) had been without sleep for three nights. Hovering in the fields outside the city waiting to dash in had been nerve wracking. Even more nerve-wracking had been the silent stealth with which the jeep had inched its way along the blacked-out streets where every creak of an opening shutter was the click of a German pistol, every doorway a potential trap. Now he was established where the routine of months of work was bearing fruit. Things were being sorted out and sifted down and he saw that the preparations had been good. Already he had coped with a few "Americans", most of whom were under lock and key by now. "Probably another vociferous Eyetie female with an uncle in Brooklyn," he thought as he looked up at the M.P. "Where is she?" he asked.

"Just over there, sir, outside the barbed wire." He looked over and I could feel a pair of dirt-rimmed green eyes appraising me. Months of semi-starvation had thinned my five-foot-ten figure and the tight, high waisted skirt I wore made me look all shoulders and hips with nothing between. I had saved my only suit for this day – a navy skirt with yellow blouse and little bolero jacket. My brown hair, from lack of sufficient grooming, had been allowed to grow to below shoulder length and was dragged back by a ribbon, setting off a pallid face with a wide mouth and large blue eyes. I was wearing make up for the first time in months and felt very conspicuous. There was no question about my being unmistakably Anglo-Saxon. My friends used to joke about my appearance at first, saying that I might just as well go about with a broad A on my forehead. When the German peril became imminent they didn't joke any more. Some of them made excuses not to walk in the street with me. Remembering this I drew myself up and looked back at the tall blond officer sitting under the tarpaulin.

The M.P. threaded his way back and pushed aside the roll of wire. "The Commander will see you now, miss," he said turning to lead the way.

The officer stood up as I approached, "Commander Lena," he said saluting. For a moment I didn't know what name to give – my married name, the name on my false ID papers, my maiden name? Seeing me hesitate he continued, "Won't you sit down? It isn't very comfortable. Our furniture two hours ago was decorating the anteroom of some Eyetie doctor's office. My official scrounger is a good lad, but he didn't know we would be entertaining or he would have brought something more suitable." He grinned and motioned to the stiff heavy wooden chair trying to put me at ease. "What can I do for you Miss...?"

"Roosevelt," I said. "Margaret Roosevelt, and I don't want you to do anything for me. I'm not here to ask for favors. I know how much of that you'll get from the Italians. I have lived here for years and it is I who would like to do something for you. I have many friends – people who want to put themselves at your disposal but are afraid of being misunderstood. I know the set-up, political and otherwise. Surely, I can be of some use. I could translate. You see, I've been in hiding during the German occupation and this is my first day out. I have friends who live in an apartment at the end of the square and they sent me to ask if you and any of your men would like to come up for a bath!"

All of this came tumbling out without my drawing breath and I don't think the commander paid much attention to any of it until he heard the word "bath". Then he sat up and took notice. "A bath sounds like heaven, Miss Roosevelt," he said. "I'll just clean up a few more details here and then with your permission I'll bring my Royal Marine driver and Major Harris, who is also attached to us, and will take advantage of your generous hospitality."

I sped away and raced back up to the apartment to tell the girls. Vittoria's fiancé, who owned flourmills, was there and had brought us some pasta – real pasta made with white flour – and we set about preparing a reception. Wine was iced and tortes were baked and spaghetti sauce was set to simmer and then we waited. Toward evening, four men arrived. The bathroom had been polished and the tub was filled with icy water, but they sloshed happily around and every fifteen minutes or so one of us would reach around the door and pass in a glass of wine. We were all keyed to an incredible pitch of excitement. Finally, the ablutions were completed and we all assembled in the dining room. There was Commander Ronald Lena, Royal Naval Volunteer Reserve; tall, blond, green-eyed and very British in his khaki shorts and blouse with epaulets. There was Major Harris of the British Army in battle dress and regimental insignia. There was Commander Lena's loyal Marine driver, Fred Hall, very stiff and formal and polite. Last of all there was a little ginger-haired fellow who didn't say very much and when he did speak the words came out so very British from between closed lips that nobody could understand him. This was Lt. Commander Crabb, known to the British as Crabby but to the Americans, naturally, as Buster. This was the same Crabb who many years later was to disappear in mysterious circumstances in Portsmouth Harbor while diving to investigate the keel of a Russian naval vessel. These men, along with assorted American naval officers, FBI men and other strange types, who appeared for a while and then as mysteriously disappeared, formed the nucleus of a counterintelligence group that had been working together in advance of the troops since before the Anzio beach head.

We gathered around the dining room table and I think that for every one of us it was the first moment of relaxation in many, many months. We ate spaghetti and fruit and we drank wine. We toasted the British and the Americans and the partisans and the Fazzari family. We toasted Papa, who had a hard time keeping his stern expression. We talked and laughed and as it grew dark we lit the candles and turned on the gramophone and danced in the twilight. The commander was taller than I and as we danced I felt as if I were floating and I wanted time to stop and I ached, trying to hold on to each minute and make it last. He told me that he was married, he told me he had a roving eye, he told me they would be moving out as soon as the job in Rome was cleaned up. I listened and I looked and I felt his arms around me and by the time the evening broke up I knew that I was falling in love.

I went home with Adelina. Somebody loaned us a jeep as it was a long way back to the vicinity of the convent where Adelina had her own apartment and there was room for me to stay until I could move back into my own home. I ached to have my own things around me again and feel free to move about. For the moment, the physical disadvantages of housekeeping didn't seem to matter. I had made a vow that if I could once again be warm enough and not be afraid all the time, I wouldn't ask anything more from life. Like most vows this was quickly modified and then replaced and then forgotten as other values came to the fore. The Germans had blown the hydroelectric plants at Tivoli on leaving so the city was without any power. We were also without gas for cooking and running water except for the little street fountains where we had to line up daily to fill our flasks and bottles. There was also no way of heating the houses, but this was not an immediate problem.

The word for the moment was rejoice, and its manifestation was parties and food. We had been adopted by Commander Lena's group as reliable "locals" and we had adopted them wholeheartedly as our liberators and friends. Nothing was too good for them. Adelina's apartment became open house – we scrounged black-market food and prepared fresh meals for them in exchange for the exquisite tins of various types of rations that they were heartily sick of but to us were novel and tasty. Their group had deserted Piazza Navona and moved to the Hotel Nazionale behind the Piazza Colonna and every day I would walk or bicycle the seven miles down to the hotel to see them, to translate documents if called upon or to give biographies of the many local people constantly turning up to offer their services. There were also lists of people who were wanted for one purpose or another and since everyone was very cagey about being winkled out of hiding, it presented quite a problem. Of course, all the big-time Fascists had followed the government and the Germans up north, but there were plenty of small fry who hoped to get in with this new group.

I shall never forget my bewilderment on the first morning when I turned into the square in front of the hotel. Six or seven American soldiers had taken up positions around the sides of the square and were all chewing gum and wearing funny little peaked cabs while they lazily tossed a ball from one to another catching it in a gloved hand. I stared goggle-eyed in astonishment and couldn't imagine what purpose gloves and balls could serve as part of a soldier's equipment.

Commander Lena had his temporary office in the main salon of the hotel. He sat behind a table with a carafe of wine and some glasses while people came and went and presented papers and the various characters of the people and the potential ability to get the city back into some kind of running order was discussed and investigated. Those who had been in hiding were seething with resentment and desire for revenge against those who had collaborated with the Germans. The latter had to be rounded up and jailed as much for their own protection as anything else. I shall never forget the morning when they found Senise, the police chief – the one who had tried to send me to a camp, but for the intervention of Ciano. The Allies tried to get him to jail, but the mob lynched him and one woman bit off his ear before they threw him off a bridge into the Tiber. On my walks across town I would occasionally see a girl sitting on a chair on the sidewalk while several other girls and boys were engaged in shaving her head. As a rule, she just sat there and cried with her face buried in her hands. I had no curiosity or sympathy with these traitors. I had my own life to re-organize.

I know it sounds trivial, but one of my greatest desires was to get my hair done! I went to my hairdresser on the via Veneto who was overjoyed at seeing me. Dear Carlo. He kissed my hand and kept exclaiming, "Signora! Signora! We were so afraid you were dead!" For the first time in my life I had my hair cut short – I was so sick of that long, stringy mess, full of olive oil and the kerosene I had used to kill the lice. When it was washed and set I joined the other ladies lined up on chairs in the sun on the via Veneto. Since of course there was no electricity for the dryers we sat and baked until it was dry enough to comb out. Afternoons I spent trying to get my apartment in the via Panama ready for me to move in. The furniture and rugs had to be resurrected and my personal belongings disinterred from my father-in-law's garden. Antonio, the portiere of my apartment building told me the details of Giuli's narrow escape.

"You and the signore had been away only a short time," he said, "when one night at midnight I was awakened by a great banging on the door. There stood two Fascist militia inquiring which was your apartment. You can imagine, Signora, my consternation. I knew the little girl was there alone with the governess, but what could I tell the soldiers? I told them you were away, but they insisted on seeing for themselves. I tried to work on their sympathies – I told them that a little girl was all alone there with a governess who was pregnant. I said if they went waving a pistol about under the poor woman's nose at that hour of the night than she would probably give birth then and there and how would they want that on their conscience? They consulted with each other and being Italians, and not Germans, and therefore sentimental, they told me they would be back at six the next morning. You can imagine, Signora! I raced up the street to the home of the Signor's mother and together we got the child to safety." He crossed himself. "God be praised signora – I was frightened to death, but fortunately there were no reprisals." Bravo Antonio – it took a real act of heroism to stand up for anybody in those days.

Gradually my home was put back together again. My beloved old cook, Ada, sought me out and my houseboy, Bruno, appeared out of nowhere. The last night I was to spend at Adelina's the usual group gathered for a party. Gemma's husband was a superb pianist and we danced and drank and sang "Lili Marlene" and "Roll Out the Barrel", which the Italians had appropriated under the title of 'Rosamunda'. By this time we had paired off Anna with Major Harris, Adelina with a tall handsome and young British naval officer known as Robbie, and myself with Commander Lena. At some point in the midst of the festivities I found myself in the kitchen with the commander. A little balcony opened off it onto a courtyard and we stepped outside. To the north the sky was lit with streaks and flashes of light where the fighting still raged as the Allies pursued the Germans toward Florence. It resembled heat lightning as it flared over the horizon, but it was too distant for us to hear and where we stood all was still. I looked up at the stars and at the distant flashes and then Ron gathered me into his arms and we kissed. For me it was as if my whole life had been waiting for that moment. I had not believed myself capable of such a rush of emotion – it was a giving and a sharing and a complete and utter dedication. In the few days that we had been together, a mounting physical desire had been growing, but we found also that we shared more than just two people thrown together by the circumstances of war. There was an almost uncanny affinity of tastes – sense of humor, appreciation of beauty, and, most binding of all, knowledge of and love for Italy. We even talked in a broken mixture of languages – it was so long since I had spoken English that expressions and phrases evaded me, and since Ron had spent his childhood in Venice it didn't take long for his fluency to return. Our lovemaking was all in Italian, which gave it a freedom and depth that neither of us could have expressed in English. For myself I wouldn't have known what to say and Ron, being British, wouldn't have known how to say it! This way we were both spared self-consciousness. That moment on the balcony was burned into my memory and when we returned to the party I was in a daze. I didn't want him to leave and I wanted to be alone with him and there was nothing I could say or do as he gathered his group and left. I would have to wait to find out if that moment had had any meaning for him. I had never believed that love could happen in so short a time, but I knew that what I felt transcended mere physical desire. The wartime morality of Roman life had made me an expert on the latter.

The next day my husband and I moved back into the apartment on the via Panama and that night the group at the Hotel Nazionale gave a party. It was a weird feeling for me to be able to talk freely with whom I pleased, to dance and laugh under the jealous glare of my husband and know that for the first time he was helpless – he could not retaliate by slapping me or dragging me away or forcing me to sit by myself and give him an account of everything I had said and had been said to me. He was afraid and he knew I could harm him if I chose to, but for me it meant only the final freedom that my own people had brought me. I was radiant with the inner happiness that consumed me – I had the secret of being in love and the continuing euphoria of long-awaited liberation. Ron and I danced and he laughed at my husband's ineffective glowering and for the first time I was able to laugh too and to see him not as my jailer, but as an ineffectual little man to be laughed at and pitied.

The group had grown and now swelled with American naval officers, Canadians, a few South Africans plus an Australian or two. I saw an American naval lieutenant sitting alone on a couch and with my new-found assurance I went over and started talking to him. He was from New York too. All of a sudden he looked at me and said, "Aren't you Marghi Roosevelt?" I said yes. "Then you must be Dodie's sister," he said. I had had no news of my family in over four years – "Yes, yes," I almost cried. "How is she?"

He looked me straight in the eyes. "She's dead," he said.

We sat there. After a few minutes Ron came over. "Let me take you home," he said. My husband and I climbed into the jeep and Ron drove us back to the via Panama. I made him come in. I didn't know what to say and I didn't want to talk to my husband. "We'll have to talk about some way to get you back to the States," Ron said. "Perhaps we can go to Naples to talk to Admiralty about it. I'll see what I can do. Will you be all right?"

He left. I refused to think about what had happened. With icy control I told my husband that the next day I was going to a lawyer to see about getting a legal separation, and then I was going to Naples with Ron to see about getting myself home. I also told him that this time he would have to leave our home – the situation had changed and I was going to stay where I was and I advised him to get a job with the Allies if he wanted to save his skin. Hierarchy in the Fascist Party was no longer an advantage.

And so it was that with the feeling that the entire 5th Army was standing squarely behind me I found the courage the next day to telephone a lawyer friend and we went down to City Hall where I obtained a legal separation from my husband. He, in turn, was accepted as a Captain Liaison Officer with a Gurkha Regiment of British 8th Army and took off for the Adriatic Front. I felt almost sorry for him – he was terrified of the Gurkhas and their long knives and since the story went that they were paid for every pair of ears they brought in, I'm sure he never knew a moment's peace or had a tranquil night's sleep. Ears look very much alike whether German or Italian!

With these details taken care of, my home and my own things around me once more and a freedom to move and say and do that I had never had before, I started living at an emotional peak that kept my head in the clouds, my feet off the ground and every nerve in between stretched as taut as a violin string. Ron had decided to report to Naples before moving north and invited me to go with him, ostensibly to discuss some means of getting me home. Across the road from my apartment was a small open field where the Americans had set up an anti-aircraft battery. The night before I was to leave for Naples I turned in early as I wanted to look well for Ron and as my nerves had made sleeping difficult I was determined to get some rest even though I had taken to leaping about in bed like a fish on the end of a hook. It felt as if every time I started to doze off with exhaustion, all my muscles would suddenly tense and I would jump a foot in the air, my eyes would fly open and I would have to start fighting off the same creeping feelings of death advancing up my body that I had battled with for so long in the convent. It usually ended up with my spending the night propped up against a pillow fighting off sleep so that whatever "it" was wouldn't get to me. This one night was even worse than usual – the anti-aircraft gun across the street never let up. Under normal circumstances the noise alone would have kept me awake, but the sound of the gun combined with the rumble of the planes drove me half crazy and by the time Ron came to pick me up in the morning I felt as if I were under anesthesia. Everything seemed far away, but at the same time colors were brighter and sounds were louder and smells were more pungent.

We took off in the jeep down the via Casilina, the inland road to Naples. The jeep was still in combat trim, i.e. windscreen down and short pole sticking up at a right angle in front. This was to intercept the wires that the Germans stretched across the roads to decapitate the driver. It was hot and windy and dusty but I was in ecstasy. Ron was in his khaki shorts and white shirt and naval cap and I watched his brown hands on the steering wheel and the authority with which he led our little convoy and I felt safe again. At noon we halted; the mines had only been cleared from about three feet on each side of the road, and so we ate our lunch sitting on the running board. I had brought bread and cheese and a bottle of wine. My face and hair and eyelashes were all coated with a reddish brown dust, but everything around us was so beautiful and fresh and new that I felt as if I was seeing the world for the first time. There is nothing as blue as the Italian sky in June before the heat of the summer washes out the color, and there is no other sight to equal the aquaducts and umbrella pines of the Roman campagna silhouetted against them.

The drive took until early afternoon and as we entered the outskirts of Naples we had to pick our way through rubble and bomb craters. The port itself was far from being cleared. Upended hulls of ships poked up like whale snouts – but the wharf area itself was busy with ships being unloaded while innumerable silver barrage balloons floated overhead. The city was crowded with refugees. Thousands of them were living in caves, in the nearby countryside and children ran in packs importuning the soldiers and selling contraband. Girls could be had for chocolate or tins of corned beef. A few years later, Roberto Murolo was to record one of the most haunting laments I have ever heard. A Neapolitan longing to return to his beloved city addresses himself to the monastery of St. Claire as he sings:

> Oh love. I want to leave tonight – I can no longer stand to be so far away, but they tell me there is nothing left, nothing but the same azure sea. Oh Monastery of St. Claire, my heart is dark – oh why, why every evening must I think of Naples as it was, of Naples as it is? My heart breaks when I hear people say that my lovely city has become corrupt. Why? No, no – it isn't true, no, I don't believe it. I long to return, but I am afraid. Afraid? Yes – if it were true, if they have told me the truth, but you, Monastery of St. Claire, enclosed within your walls, you remember how many innocent girls became brides of Christ. Now they tell me there are no more innocent girls. Oh love, I long to come back to Naples. But what can I do? I am afraid to return.

It was a sentiment I could feel but couldn't put into words. The devastation of war is easier to resist that the degradation of conquering armies.

A friend of Ron's had offered us the use of his apartment and Ron dropped me off to freshen up while he went to headquarters to report. When he returned it was dark and we stood on the balcony overlooking the bay and the city, which was still blacked out. Vesuvius had erupted only a few weeks before and a brilliant streak of lava zigzagged its way down the slope of the mountain. Together we went for dinner at one of the local restaurants, where an obliging orchestra strove to please the occupying army by playing unrecognizable American jazz. Ron and I would have preferred the classic Neapolitan tenor with his big diamond ring, but we settled for 'People will Say We're in Love', which I had never heard, but which, before the evening was, over took on a certain poignancy which still has the power to move me. We ate and we danced and we didn't talk very much and then we went back to Peter's apartment. That night we became lovers. For me it was at once for the first time and for ever. There was no past and no future and no holding back. I had never experienced love as a spiritual as well as a physical manifestation and the force of the emotion was almost more than I could bear. All at once I was overwhelmed by an entire lifetime of searching, culminating in that instant. I wept for the waste and bitterness of the past, the transience of the present and the uncertainty of the future. But most of all I wept for Ron and myself, for having found each other too late in the middle of a war, which I knew had to tear us apart. I thought that for Ron it was still only a wartime episode. Men do not give themselves so easily or with so little reservation. "Man's love is to man's life a thing apart." He was still fighting a war and there were many other things to think about. His British reserve ran smack into my Italian reckless abandon.

The next day we went to Navy House ostensibly to talk to the admiral about the possibility of some way of getting me home, even though we both knew it was premature and pretty farfetched. I was waiting in the admiral's office when an American naval officer came in. He looked familiar and I was sure I had met him somewhere. The longer I looked at him the more I was convinced that we must have known each other but I just couldn't place him. We chatted idly, but he didn't give me a clue. Finally I said, "How nice to see you again!" He mumbled something and excused himself. Ron came in just as he was leaving and I couldn't wait to ask, "Who in the world was that? I know I've seen him before!" Ron looked at me in disbelief. "That was Douglas Fairbanks Jr.," he replied.

We had to lunch at the naval mess before returning to Rome as most of the local restaurants were off limits to the military. We got into conversation with an American officer who had apparently been doing some sightseeing. He described how he had arrived at a place – a large level plain, chained off – and the Italian at the gate tried to refuse him entrance. He announced that no G..d...ed Eyetie was going to tell him where not to go so he just busted through and drove his jeep around with the Italian racing after him waving his arms and shouting. He said the place looked like it was smoking and smelled awful but since there didn't seem to be too much to see after all, he drove away. Ron and I looked at each other in horror. Without knowing it our American friend had been driving his vehicle over the crust of what is known as "little" Vesuvius, Pozzuoli. It is a crater, seamed and cracked with an occasional cone sticking up. There are pits of boiling lava and hot sulfur sand and steam caves. It is very similar to the area in Yellowstone Park and just as likely to erupt or cave in. I tried to explain the danger to our friend but he only seemed annoyed at the idea of an Italian trying to tell him what to do.

When we arrived back in Rome we found that the Italo-American members of the group had done themselves very well. They had commandeered a luxurious apartment overlooking the Tiber, a brisk black market in food had been initiated and there were all the comforts of transportation – a Lancia, a rowing shell for exercise, and we talked casually about our "yacht" and cars, even though the only gas available was at the army petrol points and the only places with electricity, running water, gas and heat were the few hotels where the army had set up auxiliary plants and which were used for "rest camps". Consequently, all of the more expensive females frequented the Excelsior and a brisk market in dope was carried out at the Grand right under the noses of the Allied Command.

Ron moved into the apartment, but his office was still at the Nazionale and every day I would bicycle down to be near him. In the evening everyone, or so it seemed, would come to my home. They brought liquor and the bar was always open. They brought food and Ada cooked up the most exquisite meals. They relaxed and danced and drank and laughed. One of the Americans, Tony T., was a natural clown and somewhat of a rogue. He was forever dreaming up get-rich-quick schemes, some of which I am sure were put into practice. The Nazionale gang – Ron, Robbie, Crabb and Major Harris with Anna, Gemma, Adelina and myself formed a permanent nucleus while British and American naval officers, South Africans, Australians, FBI men, an occasional Pole from General Anders's group and even a Brazilian or two drifted through and contributed to the excitement. Every night we danced and drank, ate spaghetti and roared with laughter when Tony performed a shadow striptease on the dining room wall. He became so famous for this that one night we even hosted a British admiral for dinner and entertainment. It was like living in a Thorne Smith novel – wild, improbable, amoral and hilarious. An Australian named Pete had found an apartment just up the street from mine and the stalwarts of the evening usually wandered up there when the liquor ran out. Pete thoroughly lived up to the reputation that the Australians had acquired among the natives. They were feared for their frenzied ways and their manner of riding rough-shod over all opposition; neither the furniture nor the women were safe when they had had a few drinks. When Ron was around, however, I had no problems – I was his girl, but despite this I could flirt and laugh and unbend in a way that had not been permitted to me in years. His presence in the background was the rock upon which I was gradually rebuilding my emotional life. Just knowing he was there freed me from self-consciousness and fear. He made no demands, but in his quiet way he made me feel I was his and the happiness was almost too much to bear. One night, coming home from Pete's, I found I had forgotten the key to the front door of my building. As usual we were far from sober. Ron was walking very deliberately on the balls of his feet and articulating with great precision while I danced ahead and around him singing Fascist songs as a gesture of defiance into the night. We circled my apartment, which was on the ground floor – but still quite a long way up, to see if we could find an open window. For some reason, Ron was carrying a silver candelabrum with four lighted candles. I stood on his shoulders and felt my way along the side of the building to find a window without shutters. I knew I couldn't crash through the heavy wooden slats of the *persiane* but I could break the glass if I had to. Finally, I discovered one of the living room windows, which hadn't been secured. I whispered to Ron to give me a heave and the first thing I knew I was lying on my stomach across the sill with my legs sticking stiffly out into the street. I swiveled my head around and there stood Ron solemnly holding the candelabrum gazing seriously up at me, and there I was on my stomach half in and half out of the window and I got the giggles. The more I laughed the less I could move and the more upset Ron became. He didn't want to be picked up by the M.P.s at three in the morning and have to explain a silver candlestick and a pair of disembodied legs. Finally, I fell into the room and went to let him in the front door.

One night, we entertained a real war hero – a British naval lieutenant by the name of Marvin Salomon. Marvin had won the DSC for some act of heroism performed during the fighting in Greece and was enjoying a well-earned breather in the fleshpots of Rome. Like so many of the British fighting men he had been overseas for five years and I often wondered if any semblance of family life would be left to these men when and if they returned home. Poor Marvin had formed an unrequited attachment for one of Rome's more notorious *poules de luxe*. She was out for bigger game so he used to come to my house to drown his sorrows. One night, he passed out cold on the living room couch. Ron and I gently removed his shoes and left him to sleep it off. The next morning as I was preparing to struggle out of bed, Ron came into the bedroom with a peculiar look on his face and asked me to please stay where I was until he gave me the word. I wondered what was going on, but waited obediently. In a few moments, Ron came back roaring with laughter. There was Marvin still fast asleep on the couch, but stark naked except for his belt! To this day, no one has figured out how he accomplished this feat and Marvin was as surprised as Ron when he woke up and found himself in that condition.

Around the beginning of July, the day I had dreaded for so long finally arrived and Ron prepared to move on. I begged and pleaded to be taken along, but Ron knew there was no place for me in what he called the ditch life, and although he wouldn't tell me where he was going he did promise that if they settled anywhere he would send for me. So began the awful period of waiting for letters. Gemma had gone to work in one of the Allied Intelligence offices so I didn't even have her to lean on during this time of waiting. Like almost all of my friends, she and her husband had separated. In Italy, where there was no divorce at that time, perhaps one of the saddest aftermaths of the war was the splitting up of families. Italian women were not equipped to earn a living, but I cannot think of a single couple that I knew in happier days that were still together after the second army of occupation had swept up the peninsular. In many cases, the women became enamoured or had a transitory affair with one of the Allied officers but mostly it was just war-weariness, strained nerves, and a feeling of defeatism and insecurity. The Italian men were on the defensive, they knew they hadn't made a very good showing and were looked down on by the Americans and British. The women had all they could do to cope with day-to-day living, food was expensive, money was scarce and everything else was practically non-existent.

Rome was one of the first testing areas for AMG (Allied Military Government) – and one of my first projects was to present for consideration the friends I knew who had been genuinely anti-Fascist and who had suffered considerably under that regime. They – and I – anticipated that naturally they would be among the first to be picked in forming a new government, running the new newspapers, re-forming the industries, etc. To my great disillusionment this was not to be the case. The same old names and figures kept popping up and being put in charge of this or that or whatever. Opportunists all – the ex-Fascists, the ones who had had money and power, now set about wooing the conquerors and winning back all their old privileges. Sick at heart I could hardly look my friends in the eyes. For years I had been saying, "Wait until the Americans come." "Wait and see how a real democracy works!" "Don't worry, the Americans will put things right when they get here!" Shamed, I could hardly believe they could be so taken in and I couldn't understand why they wouldn't listen. I also quickly found out that even though the Americans were supposedly in charge of certain departments they didn't dare make a decision until it was a okayed by the British and so I learned to turn to them whenever I needed a favor or a decision, whether it was a pass to go to Naples or the ratification of my passport to return home.

Toward the end of July, Buster Crabb turned up at my apartment with a letter from Ron. Buster was driving an enormous army lorry. He and little Giulia had formed an attachment to each other and he always managed to bring her some small gift. This time it was a stuffed mink. As always he was very formal with me – "Signora, may I take Giulia for a drive?"

"Of course, Buster," I replied and the two of them set off, Giulia's little turned up nose barely visibly through the window of the cab as she sat up straight like a little lady on her first date. I never found out how they communicated, Giuli spoke no word of English, but then even if she had she probably couldn't have understood Buster's version of the language.

Ron's letter was from Livorno – as usual his party entered one gate as the Germans retreated out the other – he wrote:

July 21, '44

Margaret darling,

Your very lovely letters arrived last night and gave me a thrill such as cannot be described on paper, but, beloved, I am glad you did not show up for never have I seen such a scene of devastation as exists here now. What war can do is well illustrated. Beloved, I hope you got the letter I sent down and that you did not find it too stiff. I get so worried about you that I didn't know which way to turn and always come up with the same points. You and I, my love, have still so much to talk about, but when I see you I shall just want to love you as always and shall not want to have any serious talk. That, however, must come later. I shall give away state secrets and tell you that I leave here tomorrow and shall try and make my way to the other place as soon as possible so that I should be back to see you on the first day of the month. Beloved, wait for me! I try hard not to be a jealous lover, but I hate to think of you with other people and I just can't help the way I feel, for you may have noticed that love does strange things to us.

We timed our entry into this place to the minute and if you realize this place fell on the 19th and we arrived on the 19th at eight forty-five in the morning. Cars and buildings were still burning but we were all okay. Things are fine, but I long to get back to you. Do you realize how many times I look at your picture and just wish and wish? I don't suppose you do. I wonder if you know that I am slow, but of the most durable type, are you beloved? Or have I judged you rightly when I say you will be a girl who after one year's arrival in the States will be in love with some other nice bloke? Darling, I am not trying to be rude, I just like to get my weird thoughts on paper and I do hope I am all wrong.

Goodnight, my love, till I write again,
Yours…

Reading between the lines I knew that from there he would try to make his way to Florence and when that city was fairly secure he would return briefly to Rome. I could have wept with relief to learn he was all right, but the parts of the letter that I hungered for was the reassurance that he loved me, and that he longed to be with me. His mind was still full of doubts as to the durability of my emotions – as he said, he was the slow type and so it was hard for him to understand my complete and swift capitulation. And so I poured out my heart in letter after letter – I told him where I went and with whom and that it was all just filling time and going through motion until we could be together. The next letter came from what he described as a "rather pleasant field near Lake Trasimeno."

25.7.44

Darling,

I am sitting in a field, rather a pleasant one and next to a lake, in fact, Trasimeno. We finished our job in Livorno and I hope now you will have my letter telling you I love you. Did I ever tell I loved you? Not from here yet! Well, I do. We got through Livorno with no trouble. My God, what a sight, it will take us a long time to put the port to work and it will take the Italians months or years to put the town back. The Germans and the Italians looted the now broken places very effectively. There was just one unfortunate incident and that was that the Germans kept aiming shells at odd moments into the town and you never knew where they were going to land. It made it a bit uncomfortable. Today, sitting in these beautiful surroundings, I've read your letters to me, three of the lovely letters one reads about and, until now, I had not yet received. But, my love, words fail me. I shall rush back to Rome soon so that at night, and when the jeeps are not crashing through the house, I can be beside you and tell you so much. Our last night in Rome was so charged with emotion and, dear God, when you talk about yourself and your past life I feel that someone is stabbing me with a knife. Then, beloved, it is human nature to creep into a hard shell and from that poor defense hurt the one you love most. Beloved, why, oh why must our lives have been so apart and why must you tell me things that cut me to my, oh so soft, heart? All the things I want to know and should not know and beloved I still however believe that you are not half as bad as you maintain. My pet, when one is bored one does some strange things but they are not done because one is vicious. The future, beloved, I leave, like a coward in the lap of those Gods who are good to us. You, I feel, must have a life in the US till you find your feet and get away from this life. Then only will you know how you stand. Be good, sweetness mine, and don't be too bored. Crabb, the darling, has a present for Giulia. I have nothing for you but my love, inadequate but sincere. There was a song when

I was last in England called "I Looked at your Picture Last Night". It was good for I look at yours each day and the time spent wanting to come to you hangs heavy. There was a line in my favorite poem, which says, "But hark! My pulse beats like a drum, telling you I come." That's me.
Goodnight love, think of me.

He was still full of the horror that had been Livorno, still under heavy shelling, the port out of commission and the town itself demolished and looted. Robbie brought the letter having come down for supplies. He told a lovely story about Buster. Buster was one of the two mine disposal experts that Ron had with him and although his activities had been mainly confined to undersea work he also helped in clearing mine fields. This was tricky work as the Shu mines were encased in wood and a regular detector was useless, plus the mines were frequently buried in layers. Somewhere Buster had picked up a pair of Italian rapiers – "liberated" from some museum no doubt – and according to Robbie he declared them far superior to the general-issue mine-detecting equipment. Robbie said it was something to see Buster striding through a minefield poking and prodding with his rapiers. Too much has been written about Crabb, particularly since his mysterious death in Portsmouth Harbor, for me to detail his exploits, but I have no doubt he was one of the bravest men I shall ever meet. His work the following winter in the harbor of Livorno, when in freezing water he personally cleared limpet mines off a great many of the sunken ships, was characteristic of the quiet heroism of which this little man was capable.

The third letter I received came from Siena. Apparently, my bombardment of passionate avowals of love and fidelity had eased Ron's mind and loosened his pen, at least to the extent of putting some of his thoughts down on paper:

Siena, 30.7.44
Darling,
I am in my seventh heaven for tonight I got five letters from you, my sweet. Four in your lovely parcel and one via Crabb. Love, do you know how I long to come back to you? Do you know how I hate this being away? You must do! I told you that I love you and the sequence is natural. I think of you and long for you, but can do nothing for I am the commanding officer and if someone can go to Rome, I cannot. Beloved, don't think of coming up, for the longest I have been in one place is four days. In Rome you can meet people even though they may bore you, but in some of these places I cannot leave you. I have slept under a roof four nights since leaving Rome. Then too, beloved, I have done 2100 miles in my jeep. I shall be back five days after Florence falls and then we shall be together. Tomorrow morning I am going from here to a few miles north of Poggibonsi and just behind the lines so we will be ready to strike. The shelling in Livorno was not nice, but none had my number.

I shall try when I get in the quietness of the country to write to you and tell you more coherently how much I love you. Beloved, try to have a good time for a few more days, then I shall come down and make myself responsible for your good time. It's getting late now and I have just lighted a candle to get a little light to finish this, my dear. Goodnight beloved, until I can come and beg you not to say goodnight but to talk to me for a while. Don't worry about life, for life is good. Hold everything till I get there and loving thanks for your loving letters, my sweet. A kiss goodnight.

Our last night together in Rome had been so charged with emotion that I love you and I love you and I love you had been everything there was to say. Now we were both having time to think. The separation was torture and we each dealt with it in our own way. Ron had his work – I was bored and desperate and seeking diversion. I could pour out my heart on paper and my thoughts about the future were all black and despairing. Ron, being an optimist, didn't want to face the future, and I should have picked up my clue from a phrase in one of his letters. "The future, beloved, I leave like a coward in the lap of those Gods who are good to us." He never did spell cut what he meant and I didn't believe I merited any particular attention from a "good" God. Miracles can happen, but they usually need a push.

The nightly orgies at my home continued – the faces and uniforms changed, but the dancing and drinking went on night after night until dawn. Looking back, I am amazed at how well behaved they all were in comparison to the all-Italian parties that used to take place before the Germans moved in on us. For some time a tall, good-looking, dark-haired Irish commander in the British Navy had been coming to join us in the evening. He usually brought a bottle and was always very correct and proper and never seemed to be having a good time or join in the fun. This had the effect of dampening the spirits, particularly of the junior officers. One evening he and I were waltzing together. He looked down at me from his six-foot-four height and in that rather superior and condescending manner that some Britishers seem to be born with, he asked, "Signora, do you reverse?"

I hesitated, and then I thought, Oh hell, it's now or never, let's find out of he has a sense of humor. I looked up as demurely as I could and murmured, "Oh commander. What a question to ask a lady." There was a slight pause and then he broke into roars of laughter and the ice was finally broken. Subsequently, he told a delicious story on himself. At the age of eighteen his family had sent him from the ancestral castle to spend a year in London to acquire polish and finesse in the ways of the big city. When the year was up he thought it appropriate to arrange a dinner at Claridge's for the people who had befriended him during his stay. He left the menu to the maître d'hôtel and after a sumptuous repast arrived the pièce de resistance – crèpes suzettes. The maître arrived with his little chafing dish and all the ingredients and prepared to start the complicated ritual. Mike looked incredulously at what was going on and then he rose up in righteous indignation. "Where I come from," he roared, "we prepare the food in the kitchen before we serve it. You take that right back and don't bring it out to us until it's ready to eat!"

One day, while I was at the Nazionale waiting to see if any mail had come in from the field, I noticed a terrific flap among the officers. Everyone was dashing about and particularly the Americans seemed bewildered and consumed with curiosity. It seems that someone had spotted a five-star general at the Grand Hotel and no one knew quite what to do about him. Motorcycle-escorted black limousines dashed back and forth between the hotel and the railroad station and up and down the via Nazionale to the Piazza Venezia. But who was he? Finally, the word trickled down to us. Marshal Tito of Yugoslavia! Since this didn't mean anything to me I only wondered how come a Yugoslav partisan was all tricked out in an American uniform – with five stars yet!

In August, Ron's letters began to sound hopeful that Florence might soon fall and that he would come back to me.

1.8.44

Mara darling,

Your lovely letters nos. 1, 2, 3 and 4 plus the one that you added via Crabb have been read and reread and I shall read them again. My dear, you fill your letters so nicely that I feel ashamed of my short notes, though the tenor of mine is similar to yours. I love you, what a nice feeling to think I shall come back. Beloved, if you do not go to the US (and I think you should) you must later come to Florence where I suppose I shall have to live. I can't stay away from you for weeks at a time. So we shall talk, during the long night watches, my love, talk of all that concerns us and us only. Are you still going out nights with assortment of funny people? I am glad, in my mean way, that you are bored. Don't do anything drastic to get rid of me for, beloved, as far as I am concerned, I hurt easily, and if the time comes when I must get the "bird" then do it verbally, then do what you wish, for then I can work my salvation in sorrow rather than have a broken inside. Why do people in love get so serious? I suppose it's because it means so much.

I hope my office is drawing you rations for the house. I shall be with you soon and so will take care of that. I love you, it hurts to be away so long.

I haunted all of the Allied officers and sent letters with anyone willing to take them. The theme was always the same – how much I loved him, how lost I felt without him, how afraid I was of going haywire when he wasn't around. This last disturbed him greatly. I had told him about the breakdown in morality when the war began – if I had loved my husband perhaps I wouldn't have been so wild. But I was snatching at life with both hands when it seemed there might not be too much of it left and gradually all accepted moral standards became meaningless. Only someone who has lived through it can understand the *dolce vita*. It wasn't for kicks or in protest or for escape or even in defiance. Things were that way and so they became the way of life. Falling in love had thrown a monkey wrench into my mental wheels and although the old life still seemed normal I began to feel guilty about it. I tortured Ron with details of my activities because I wanted to force the reassurance of his love, but only when I was with him did I find any kind of normal communion.

His letters talked of bringing me to Florence to be with him so that we could talk during the night watches of all that concerned us and us only. As commanding officer he couldn't get away and even in Rome our privacy was a precious thing to be stolen in snatches at night and, as we expressed it jokingly when the jeeps weren't crashing through the house. Interspersed with his expressions of worried jealousy and ardent affection was a very real picture of how his part of the war was going. On August 7, he wrote:

> *We are sitting in south Florence and the Germans are paying no attention to the BBC news that the place has been captured. So they keep throwing a lot of stuff over and in fact it's quite hot. You still love me? By the way, there are no bridges left except the Ponte Vecchio and that is mostly blocked at each end by two houses the Germans just brought down to make sure we would not get in. Beloved, I long for you and think of you and wait for you. Kill the fatted calf, for your prodigal is coming home!*

But it was not to be. On August 17, he wrote:

> *Dearly beloved,*
> *It is now 9:15 o'clock and therefore by our standards late. We are having what one might call a bad time for we are in a Florence which we are sharing with the Germans, albeit*

unwillingly. Only three hours ago I watched the Germans put six shells into a building, which was quite clearly marked with a Red Cross. The shelling goes on all the time and it has a tendency to make one a bit jittery. Beloved, it doesn't make me feel quite as bad as that horrible feeling I get from your letters, which, God help me, I love, not the horrible feeling, the letters. Your very first tells me that you are suffering from, shall I say, going "haywire". Please, please don't tell me that in these parties, which you have to go to only because you are bored you finally, out of that same boredom, give yourself to whatever bloke you happen to be out with? Darling, I am very male, with all the male weaknesses but don't tell me that, for while in my heart of hearts I feel you don't, love makes me unreasonable. I only feel that I love you enough to play it straight as I can, if I don't hurt your feelings play it the other way if that's the way WE want it; I personally don't; when I fall for a girl like you it can only happen to me once, and it has happened to me now with you, I therefore can't compromise. My character, as far as women go, is not strong, only because in the main I am too lazy, indifferent and as I told you liquor is my hobby. Love comes along and knocks the hell out of all that but because of that I go moral and while my roving eye continues I play it straight. Honey, all this I feel in my heart, does not apply to us. But being a stereotype lover, I hate the idea, not of your going out having a good time, but of your going out, staying out from sheer boredom. I can condone someone falling for someone, but not playing. Oh, Hell, why am I so wet? I think I am bomb happy for when we get a few hours respite I think of holding you in my arms and it's a joy but provokes discontent. Today is the 17th and I feel we shall clear this town soon and I give you my promise to be in Rome before next Sunday week. Did I tell you I have had the good fortune to be recommended for the third highest US decoration? I shall probably never know why or shall probably not get it, but being a male, and therefore male vanity sets in, I am pleased. When male vanity sets in, beloved, I feel that you must be nuts *to fall for me but oh beloved I love it and I love you. I feel quite lost when I think of you for when I think of you I must have you many miles away and that is just where I don't want you. You must excuse my poor letters, but what with machine guns and shells and only a candle, I can't help smiling for I am in the Excelsior and I had many good nights here when the people were all dressed up and very Bryn Mawr and oh so young and, may I say, easy! Now it is not the same, there are so many young snipers and the consequent bodies lying around the streets, for the Germans control most of the corners and one cannot rescue others. Buster is here and happy, what a strange affection he has for little Giulia, nearly as strong as I have for Giulia's mother.*

Oh honey! It won't be long now. I have pictured my return to Rome as a hero, as a naval officer and as a lover, accept me as one of the last two for the first was just my day and night dreaming. Goodnight love.

Finally, the day came. This time there was no question about lodgings – Ron moved in with me and for the first time in years there was a happy household in via Panama. Old Ada worshipped the "Signor Commandante" as she watched the change in me and although the hectic entertaining continued, when the apartment finally grew quiet at night we were alone, and we would stand on the little terrace and listen to the nightingales calling to each other from the pines in the Villa Felicetti across the street, bathed in moonlight and peace. In the stillness and the long night hours we talked of our love, but most of all we held each other in a complete communion of spirit which needed no words. For a brief period we could cast off the aura of uncertainty and sadness and live in the present, which was so precious and which we both knew in our hearts was all we were to have.

It was arranged that I would accompany Ron to Florence. I had a quasi-legitimate reason, but we couldn't bear to be separated even at the cost of jeopardizing his career. We were both aware of the innuendo, the invidiousness and poison that might result, but we weighed the risk and found it worth it. As always the poison eventually won out, but I can honestly say that neither of us cared.

While Ron worked out the details and obtained a pass for me, I arranged for Giuli to go back to her grandmother's. It lacked only a few days to our departure when one early morning Ada burst into the bedroom almost hysterical, "*Signora mia!*" she cried, "*venga a vedere, ci hanno rubato tutto!*" Ron and I stumbled out of bed. We had forgotten to pull down the heavy wooden shutters leading to the terrace the night before and "*ci hanno rubato tutto*" with a vengeance. Every bit of silver, jewelry and object of value that I possessed had disappeared. All the flat silver, all the wedding presents, all the family antiques that I had brought from New York and that had been hidden so painstakingly from the Germans – gone without a trace. Perhaps I had been foolish to bring them back, but I had so longed to have my own things around me again – to see the sideboard in the dining room gleaming with the silver tea and coffee set that had belonged to my grandmother and the candlesticks that Bruno took such pride in polishing. We found jeep tracks under the window and we went to the Italian police but they just shrugged. Italian authorities still had very little authority. I took the loss philosophically. I was sorry, of course, but there wasn't time then to sit down and mourn about it.

Ron had to get back to Florence and at last all was

ready, my pass made me a bonafide member of his intelligence group and one morning early in September we set off in his jeep. Over the Ponte Milvio we went with the yellow Tiber low in its banks beneath, and out the gate onto the via Flaminia. The road was in fair condition and we made good time. The Allied advance from Rome to Florence had been so swift that aside from the usual litter of burned-out trucks and broken-down tanks that lined the margins, it was practically an autostrada compared to the fought-over stretch from Naples north where the towns were bombed-out husks and the mines had been cleared from only a few feet on either side of the highway. We made good time, through Viterbo, stopping to sample a bottle of Est-Est-Est at Orvieto where we entered the gentle Umbrian country-side. Here the big, white, placid oxen still ploughed the fields and the green hills rolled away into the distance melting into olive orchards. Then we started the climb into the mountains and through the pass called Radicofani, which dropped us down onto the Tuscan plain near Siena and then it was downhill all the way to Florence.

The gang was gathered at the Excelsior. Robbie was there, and a very young Canadian paratrooper who had been attached to Ron's group named Tourneau, and a rather weird RNVR lieutenant whose mother had obviously had one of those love affairs with Florence so common to the turn-of-the-century Englishwomen, as he was called, so help me, Michelangelo O'Hara! They were all drinking an original concoction, which Ron and I had popularized and which consisted of one half Italian brandy and one half sweet Italian vermouth – of course, without ice. It was quick in its affect and there was plenty of it, which was about all you could say for it. The accommodation problem had not yet been solved but one of the JAG's bright young men following the black market up from Rome kindly offered Ron and me the use of his apartment until the group found permanent lodging. His flat was on the top floor of an old villa looking out over the city. It was already dusk when we arrived, having picked up supplies. I was exhausted and over-excited and swept by waves of creeping suffocation which I tried frantically to stem by drinking and keeping on the move. Florence in September is still breathless – hot and steamy, it sits like an old-fashioned jewel sunk in its setting of surrounding hill towns. I climbed out onto the roof and set up a card table where I placed a candle, a bottle of wine, a tin of corned beef and some bread. We lugged some beautifully carved chairs out and sat down for dinner with the Arno winding below us and the usual flashes of gunfire lighting the horizon in the distance. In spite of the heat the night had a feeling of velvet all around us and the two of us up on the roof with the candle between us found a world where no one else belonged. It was another one of those rare moments in which all the senses are heightened and one knows that it will only be lived through once and therefore it must be made to last, each second stretched to eternity, each smell, touch, sensation savored slowly and captured consciously. We went to bed, but neither of us could sleep. My nerves were too raw and my whole body twitched involuntarily and each time I dozed off through sheer exhaustion the suffocating feeling returned and forced me to return to consciousness. I could feel Ron tossing and turning beside me and I knew he was worried about bringing me to Florence and about what the consequences might be, but I didn't dare talk about it for fear he would send me back.

The next morning Robbie turned up with the glorious news that he had found a villa, which he had promptly sequestered for our group. Not only that, he had found us a cook, one Celestin, who had been a chef at Doney's, one of Florence's more chic coffee houses, a counterpart of Rosati's in Rome and Gerbeau's in Budapest. The villa was in via Ciro Menotti, and from the inventory must have been inhabited by elderly Englishwomen. I never saw so many old-fashioned whalebone drawstring corsets in my life. However, we meticulously listed everything, locked all personal possessions in a room and repaired to the Excelsior where we had lunch – the theory being that I would spend the afternoon cleaning the villa while the men pursued their hush-hush activities. They dropped me off at the front door, waved goodbye and the jeep drove away. The front door opened onto a foyer and a flight of stairs leading to the main door of the villa. To this door they had forgotten to give me the key. There was no way to get in. I climbed out of a window from the landing hoping there would be some way to get to the living-room window. From what I could see the blinds were down. There was about a three-inch ledge running underneath the windows and I wondered if I would have enough courage to inch myself along it and try the windows. The one-storey looked awfully high off the ground. I sat there with my legs dangling over the side of the building, willing myself to try it, cursing Robbie for not giving me the key, and wishing I weren't quite so full of vino and cognac–vermouth. For over two hours, I fought and argued with myself. Every time I lowered myself onto the little ledge and tried a few steps, I realized there was nothing to hold on to and scrambled back into my window seat. So there I sat brooding and watching the neighbors who in turn, I soon found out, were watching me. About 4.30, I heard the sound of fire engines, which came closer and closer until finally, hook and ladder and all came around the corner and stopped directly under my window. Up came the ladder and up came a Florentine fireman. I tried to be dignified but it was pretty difficult.

"The Signora is in trouble?" he asked.

"No," I said.

"Why is the Signora sitting on the window ledge?" he asked.

"Because I like it," I replied.

"The neighbors don't like it," he said. "They called us to find out what is the matter."

"There is nothing the matter," I said feeling more and more like the village idiot.

"Then will the Signora please go back inside?"

"Certainly I will if it bothers the neighbors," I replied with what dignity I could muster and since he was not about to descend the ladder or leave until I had complied I swirled about as gracefully as I could and promptly fell off onto the landing. Drawing myself up I returned to the window, thanked them for their concern, assured them that I had a legitimate right to be there and that shortly the British army would arrive to rescue me. They hung about for a bit, but I kept away from the window and they had no sooner left than the men came back, hot and dirty, expecting no doubt a tidy home away from home and dinner bubbling on the stove. I was almost in tears and when we finally entered the apartment it looked dirtier and smaller that I had remembered. However, everyone was very nice and we all had a few belts and decided to go back to the Excelsior for dinner and cope with the sleeping arrangements later. The cognac–vermouth hour stretched out into the usual tasteless PX dinner and by the time we boarded the jeep to return home we had all forgotten where it was we were headed – in fact, Robbie was the only one who even remembered the name of the street. With Royal-Marine driver Fred at the wheel we rushed through the narrow streets singing "Roll Out the Barrel" and "Lily Marlene" and every time we emerged into a piazza Robbie arbitrarily pointed Fred toward just any road heading out of it. After a while we realized we were getting nowhere and although I had never really believed that if you are lost you tend to go in circles, all of a sudden I noticed that we had passed the same American MP station three times.

I suggested we pull in and ask for directions. Fred drew up with a flourish and Robbie leaned out toward the gum-chewing policeman who approached us. "I say, old boy," bellowed Robbie, "can you tell us where we are?"

The MP bristled. "What outfit are you?" he asked suspiciously.

"British Navy, old boy," said Robbie cheerfully.

The American moved closer and gave us a long look. "And just what is the British Navy doing in Florence, sir?" he added, seeing gold braid glint on a cap in the faint light.

Robbie leaned further out toward the MP. "Looking for a battleship!" he confided in a loud whisper. I giggled and Ron gave me a stern look.

The M.P. retired to his command post and presently returned with a friend. "Where do you want to go?" the newcomer asked.

"Home," said Robbie.

"And where is that?" the new one asked again.

"We don't know!" we all said in chorus and burst into roars of laughter. This was not considered funny and all of a sudden I had the feeling we might be arrested as Nazi spies or something, when Ron decided to intervene. He slowly dismounted and with great deliberation approached the two men. He cut an authoritative figure, as the more he had had to drink the more precise he became, the slower he moved and the more an air of command he assumed. I heard snatches of the muted conversation during which I could distinguish "lend lease", "gallant allies" and the clincher "President Roosevelt". The upshot was we were offered a motorcycle escort and after a good deal of backing and filling we set off – the trim, broad-shouldered, neatly dressed Americans, their white helmets gleaming in the darkness, riding proudly erect before and behind the jeepful of rather intoxicated, undoubtedly battle-strained motley crew of British Naval officers, Canadian paratrooper and one secretary, civilian, female, me. Round and round we went again, Robbie shouting encouragement until suddenly we turned a corner and there we were – via Ciro Menotti. But our escorts were not yet satisfied. They had seen us home, now they would see us into our house and safely off the streets.

We disentangled ourselves from the jeep and waited for someone to unlock the outer door. Everyone looked at everyone else. No one had a key. The Americans moved in and from escorts they became to look more like captors. "Let me try bashing it with something," suggested Robbie, and before we could stop him he was hammering away with an iron bar. Heads popped out of windows and loud Italian complaints rent the night air. Ron shut them up – not politely. They were not to forget too soon that he had fought their battles for them. Thank God the lock gave almost immediately. We invited the two Americans upstairs, produced the key to the inside door and ushered them into the dusty stuffy apartment. We found some glasses in the dining room and Robbie pulled out a couple of bottles of brandy and before long we were toasting Allied solidarity, 5th Army, 8th Army, the British Navy, President Roosevelt and once more the strains of "Roll Out the Barrel" assaulted the languid Florentine night. We thanked the Americans and they left in the best of spirits and roared away on their motorcycles and we all fell into our improvised beds, after one of the longest and most complicated days of our pixilated Thorne Smith existence.

The next morning, Celestino arrived to take up residence and together he and I made our villa come alive. It was nicely laid out. There was a large dining room overlooking a garden where the morning sun streamed in, typical cheap Italian blond wood furniture, but comfortable and homey. Across the hall was the master bedroom with twin beds where Ron and I slept. There was a huge desk where I worked at my translations. There were two other bedrooms, one for Robbie and one shared by Tourneau and Mike (as Michelangelo O'Hara came to be called), a spacious kitchen at one end of the hall for Celestino who went home at night, a sleeping cubby hole for the Marine driver next to it, and the communal bathroom at the other end of the hall.

Robbie was assigned the job of feeding our group and

drew rations from the British DID (no one ever found out what the initials stood for) and since they refused to issue any for a party of less than sixteen people we never lacked for anything except coffee, which we purchased on the black market. With Celestino to prepare our meals we ate like gourmets and gave parties with reckless abandon. Our favorite guests were from the British 6th Armored. Sir John Marling was one of them and he and his friends were frequent dinner companions. After dinner we would settle down to a little serious drinking, which usually ended up in a wild game of "conkers". I had not been familiar with this British game of chestnuts on a string in which the opponents alternately tried to smash each others chestnuts. It sounds harmless enough, but when you find yourself steadying your chestnut opposite a khaki-clad six-foot tank driver taking serious deadly aim you soon find out that the ricochet can be bruising, since it was not sporting to waver or wince. I usually emerged from these encounters black and blue with sprained fingers and once even a quite respectable shiner. By the end of the evening the dining room was inches deep in chestnut shavings and we were all hysterical with laughter and quite breathless and not too sober and everything was fun and friendly and the war seemed for the time to have been shoved into the background.

The only fly in the ointment was Michelangelo O'Hara. He took no part in our revelry, absenting himself on his own business, which we began to suspect booked no good for our unorthodox way of life. He didn't fit into the group, he resented me and was jealous of Ron. We knew he was maneuvering some kind of dirty work and I knew that Ron would eventually have to send me back to Rome – even if only temporarily – if Mike succeeded in really stirring things up. One evening I was alone in the villa – the men had all been invited to some Canadian mess party and Celestino had gone home. It was late and I was getting ready for bed when there was a ring at the downstairs street door. I went to answer it. I opened it and there on the threshold stood Mike swaying slightly. He fixed me with his blue eyes which had a white ring around the iris and said very clearly and distinctly, "Mara, I'm pissed as a coot." Then he fell flat on his face on the foyer floor. I tried dragging him up the staircase but his head kept bumping and I didn't want to be responsible for making him any weirder that he was already so I just left him. I knew one of the men would stumble over him and get him to bed.

With the exception of Mike all was harmony in our little household. Robbie worshipped Ron and was fiercely loyal to him and if the others had any criticism or resentment of my presence they didn't voice it. On the other hand, it was pretty SOP. Most senior officers were accompanied by "secretaries", acquired locally. As for me I felt I was adding a long-postponed service and for the first time in my life I had such a complete emotional fulfillment that I didn't dare analyze it or think beyond the moment. At night while Ron slept I forced myself to stay awake and look at him and I thought, if I were a religious person and truly believed in God, I would say my prayers to you.

We had been settled in our villa for several weeks. Things were beginning to quieten down and sort themselves out. The Germans were making for Bologna and the Gothic Line, Allied Military Government was setting itself in business, the resident troops were getting organized and the natives were beginning to rebuild their homes and their lives and some were prudently starting to plan for the coming winter which promised to be, to put it mildly, uncomfortable. Artistic treasures were being brought out of hiding and the museums were opening again. To celebrate the return of peace and order the Florentines rounded up as many members as were left of their symphony orchestra and decided to give a concert in the great hall of the Palazzo della Signoria.

Ron was passionately fond of music – I knew very little about it in spite of having been dutifully exposed to opera and the Roman musical season, more, I confess for the social side than from an appreciation for music. The program was Grieg's Piano Concerto, which I had never heard, and an American GI was guest pianist. The concert was on a Sunday afternoon and the medieval, high-ceilinged stone chamber was crowded with men in uniform. I went to please Ron – but from the moment the first notes sounded, dum dum de dum dum, I was transported into another world. To my uncritical ear it was the most beautiful thing I had ever heard and my emotions soared with the music and the melody and Ron and Florence and the unutterable relief of no more bombing transposed my spirit into a state of exaltation that can still conjure up and relive, and the scene is as vivid in my mind as if it were yesterday. I was grateful for my lack of musical sophistication which enabled me to take an American soldier playing the piano with a hastily thrown-together group of musicians and turn it into something very close to heaven. I believe that the orchestra too, as well as the audience, was caught up in this mystic unity to produce a quasi-religious experience that was deeply felt. When it was over and the tension relaxed it was like a catharsis. Just for one afternoon this disparate group had been brought together in spiritual reciprocity.

The golden days of October were beginning and slowly the Arno was filling with the autumn rains from high in the mountains. Ron decided we needed another jeep and Robbie cheerfully volunteered to go to Caserta to draw one. He took off early one morning expecting to be back the following evening, but no Robbie. Instead, on the third morning we received a telephone call from the naval hospital in Livorno. It was Robbie. "What the hell are you doing in Livorno?" I asked. "Ron will be furious, we expected you back last night."

"Had a bit of a smash, old girl," he said cheerfully. "Tangled with a six wheeler coming down a hill this side of Poggibonsi."

"My God! Robbie," I said, "are you hurt? How did it happen?"

"Afraid we're out the jeep," he replied, "couldn't find the brake pedal, but I'm all right, just shaken up a bit." Gradually, I got the story out of him. Robbie didn't know how to drive! An American M.P. had put it in gear for him in Naples and he had just taken off. How he had gotten almost to Florence was a near miracle, but of course the roads were empty except for army traffic, and fairly level until he came to the hill which proved his nemesis. His optimism, however, was short-lived as he was detained for several weeks in hospital for observation. This was a severe blow to Ron. Robbie had been his mainstay and his safety valve. Then the other shoe fell. It was made clear in no uncertain terms that it would be "expedient" for me to return to Rome. The powers that be were to have a meeting in Florence to evaluate the situation and the head of each group was to attend and report.

Ron drove me down to Rome. It was a sad trip. Autumn is always a sad time. He dropped me off at my apartment. "I'll see you soon, love," he promised. "I'll sneak in and out and no one will know." He climbed back into his jeep and I watched him drive up the via Panama, Fred sitting alongside of him, and I would have given the rest of my life to have been in Fred's place.

Antonio stopped me as I was entering the hall. "The signore lives here now," he said. "Your things have been moved." I was stunned. Moved? I knew that my husband had rented a villa when we separated, but I had never been there. Why had he switched? As the winter wore on it became all too apparent. We had quite a scene, but the upshot of it was that I retired defeated to via di Villa Albani where my beloved Ada was waiting for me.

The villa was two stories set in a damp garden with white pebbled paths and a goldfish pond, from which spouted a forlorn green-bronze urchin holding a kidney-shaped sack. In normal times it had been a fountain, but the shortage of water had long since stopped the flow. To the left was the caretaker's cottage nestling beside an evil-smelling rabbit hutch. Giant palms rose out of small circular plots of earth obscuring the view from the south side, shutting out the sunlight and tapping their fronds eerily against the bedroom windows. The bedroom on the second floor was upholstered in heavy lilac brocade, and in one corner a stained glass window shed a sebaceous gloom down the length of the room. It was a bit like sleeping in a chapel. Moisture oozed through the floor and swelled and cracked the parquet strips into little hillocks, which exploded with a sharp report when stepped on – like a bubble bursting leaving the liver-colored tile gaping through the fissure. It made navigating in the dark very difficult, and it seemed to get dark very early that winter in Rome. By four thirty in the evening, night had begun to set in and the one candle stub that I shared with old Ada seemed very inadequate. That was before I stole a hurricane lantern from an officer's mess, after which I could sit loftily in the dining room by myself, freezing while Ada huddled over the charcoal burner in the kitchen. Rome suffered from a lack of everything. No gas, no electricity, water had to be fetched in flasks and bottles from the street fountains, no heating for the houses. Ada cooked over a kind of hibachi. She would stand over it and flap a fan furiously to ignite the few bits of wood and lignite that burned the eyes. There was no proper coal, no candles, queues blocks long for food and unless one was in line at dawn the supply ran out after one had been standing for hours. Darling Ada, I didn't realize what I was putting her through but she would have died rather than ask her Signora for help. So I sat at home like a lady and was miserable while she wore out her poor old feet tramping through the streets for food and standing in line for water.

The nautical atmosphere of the house was augmented by a deficiency in the plumbing system, causing the air to moan through the pipes day and night with a sound like a ship's ventilator and inspiring various Naval friends to remark that it was exactly like being in the wardroom of a destroyer.

The bathroom led directly off the bedroom and in the six months that I lived there I never got into the tub as there was no way to heat water. Washing consisted of standing in front of the basin hunched under a fur coat which I futilely tried to keep from slipping off my naked shoulders while I dabbed in a couple of inches of tepid water painstakingly heated over the charcoal burner. Even that slight concession to cleanliness was a risk in the tomblike atmosphere and served more as a sop to an Anglo-Saxon conscience than the fulfillment of any physical requirement. And so my body sat in the villa in via Albani 26 Rome, while my heart stayed in via Menotti 18 in Florence. I wrote letters to Ron, unhappy and unsure letters I'm afraid, and I waited for word from him. We had to depend on people going back and forth as the field post office took a month and with Robbie laid up there was no one in Ron's group he could trust. I was in agony to return to Florence and it all depended on the meeting and what would be decided about Ron's future. The first letter was reassuring in one way, disappointing in another. He wrote:

Sweet Margaret, someone will take this down for me, and so I sit here with so much to say and lacking words to say all that seems compressed within me.

Shall I start at the beginning and tell you how troubled and sad I felt when I with the two pongos left? We had a good, but oh so cold trip up; by 6:30, it was dark and we had passed Radicofani. We stopped to let the pongos put on sweaters and by 9:15 we arrived in Florence, just six hours after leaving Rome, and proceeded to have about six or ten brandies, which brought back the old bloodstream to normal, but I felt as if the world really had nothing to offer. I started for bed; it was then I found the conkers and the note of farewell you had put in the pocket of my dressing gown. My dear, it was devastating, one of those things that happens only once in a lifetime.

Florence, my dear, has been hell without you. I feel as if a great part of me was missing; as the Frenchman said, "to part is to die a little."

Beloved, you must try to get yourself home, where I shall come to you and hope that you have found a new happiness. I know it is foolish, but I have never in my life had so much happiness as I have since I met you, but I feel as if a relentless fate were directing me to some place where you cannot follow. But if we should meet in some place like New York then I would love to have you tell me you had found a new life.

Goodnight, love, my room is now a very lonely place and the bed opposite a reminder of paradise lost.

Then a few days later number two arrived.

Well, my love, the wolves gathered here and I must confess I found them to be veriest lambs. I have been put up for the Legion of Merit in the US which helped, I think. However, I can't have you back here love, not for a while. You must know beloved, how I hate life here or any other place without you. Florence is an unhappy place when you are not there, but possess your soul in patience for I shall get to Rome soon. Robbie is not to be returned to me, they are cutting everybody down so that fifty per cent of the staff here now will be gone in a few months time. I would like to be able to give you my plans, but as you know the usual has occurred, you get a vague idea and no more. My orders are to do the two towns, which I am waiting for and then report back to Caserta. Beloved, don't get too blue in Rome and try to eat properly. Go out and try and have some fun. You and I know how we feel about each other and I will understand. In a few days, perhaps next week, I'll drop in on you in secret.

Go out and have some fun! I didn't know where to start. I had cut myself off from most of my Italian friends. Gemma was working and living at home with her father, having separated from her husband. Most of my other friends were in the same boat. As a matter of fact, only one couple among our group remained together and since in Italy there was no divorce the heartache and readjustment is hard to understand. This, plus the fact that Italian women of that generation and upbringing had never worked and had no idea how to go about supporting themselves. Many of them became the mistresses of Allied officers, but this was tacitly accepted as temporary.

When I realized that it might be some time before I could get back to Florence I took Giuli back with me. She was still at her grandmother's and going to school at the Sacred Heart Convent at Trinita dei Monti – the head of the Spanish Steps. For a while we were company for each other. The separation had been good for both of us. She would sit at the dining-room table and do her homework by candlelight. It was hard for her to hold a pen as her hands were so covered with chilblains that she wore thick woolly gloves. My heart ached as I watched her little blond head bent over her books and the slow clumsy progress of the pen across the paper. I thought of all we had been through together and how awful I had been to her at times and then I would cry and cry and not be able to stop. Finally, I could stand it no longer. We both had colds and I was afraid she might become seriously ill. I had had one bout of pneumonia and didn't want another for either of us particularly, as in those days there was no specific medicine – the first time I had been subjected to linseed poultices until my back was so blistered that I could no longer stay in bed. I decided to put her in the convent to board. She was much happier and better off as they had heat and much better food than I could provide.

One day on the via Veneto I bumped into an old friend of mine – Prince Marcello. During our conversation I learned that he had acquired a luxurious apartment with – of all things – running hot water! He invited me over for a bath anytime. We set a weekly date for the late afternoon – bath *and* dinner. It sounded like heaven as I knew the dinner would be gourmet and I didn't give a damn what I had to do to get it. I set off at about six in the evening with a little suitcase containing clean underwear, soap and towels. Marcello let me in, showed me to the bathroom and I spent the most wonderful hour. It was heaven. It was bliss. I was warm all the way through to the bone and I soaked and bubbled and scraped little rolls of dead skin off my ankles and shoulders and emerged parboiled and weak, but warm for the first time since August. Marcello had a dinner waiting that I can remember to this day – caviar, lobster, little Roman peas cooked with bacon, and endive salad. The light white wine I loved. We ate and talked and when we had finished he put some more wine on ice and dismissed the manservant. This is what I had been expecting and I thought I'd just play it by ear, but when the pitch came it was from an entirely different quarter than the one I was braced for. It wasn't sex, it was cocaine. Like so many people in Rome at that time Marcello was a sniffer. What used to amuse me was that the headquarters for the dope traffic was in the Grand Hotel – which was also the Allied Headquarters. At any rate, sniffers are a bore because they won't let you alone – I had been through this with my husband. They sniff, everybody must sniff. Maybe it's because the Italians didn't drink that they had to get their kicks some other way. As for me, I was too fond of wine and I was apprehensive about cocaine. So it went until three in the morning – long after curfew. I sipped wine and Marcello kept urging me to try "just one sniff". Every time I tried to leave he would grab me and become upset and I would sit down again and the argument would start all over. Finally, I managed to get out and by dodging through the streets and back ways made my way home without being stopped. But I was worn out. I only tried one more bath, but it was the same story plus I was sighted by a patrol and shot at when I ran so I decided that it wasn't worth it.

The days and nights dragged wearily on. I went out occasionally, but without Ron I was hollow. All the sparkle of life had gone out of me and I was bored, bored, bored by other people. Restless and unhappy I searched for ways to return to Florence. I haunted the various Allied offices trying to get a permit to travel north, but I couldn't come up with what they considered a valid excuse for going and I didn't dare compromise Ron by mentioning his outfit. Half of the battle had been won, however; I had a place to stay. A friend of mine lived out near the Mugnone River, a part of Florence that had been very thoroughly bombed, and her house was still in a partially destroyed state. Doors and windows were lacking and most of the furniture had been ruined or stolen, but there were two compensations. The Allies had set up a temporary power plant so that there was electricity, and my friend Antonia had managed to close off a room which had a fireplace and which she said I could use. Wood was hard to find, but since I had introduced her to our little group in via Menotti our able scrounger, Robbie, had managed somehow to provide. Antonia was a very attractive woman – she was also sentimental and she thought it a crime that Ron and I should be kept apart. So I bombarded Ron with letters imploring permission to come and promising not to cause him embarrassment.

Things were hanging fire like this when one day I was invited to lunch by a British colonel whom we had nicknamed "Poonah". It was a logical choice. He was with an Indian regiment, sported a large ginger mustache and had a habit of blowing out his cheeks as if saying "harroomph". He also had a monocle. Having nothing better to do I accepted and ate a hearty lunch. Returning home about four I fell onto the bed with all my clothes on and promptly fell fast asleep. The next thing I knew old Ada was shaking me and exclaiming excitedly, *"Signora, c'e il Commandante! Il Commandante e arrivato!"* I stumbled to my feet and ran to the little balcony in the front of the house. There, outside the gate were Ron, Robbie and the driver sitting in their jeep grinning and honking the horn. I rushed downstairs and fell into Ron's arms, crying as if my heart were broken and exclaiming, "I haven't been to bed all night!" I was half afraid that he would wonder at my being fully clothed at what I thought was the crack of dawn. I finally untangled myself and realized it was cocktail not breakfast time and we all repaired to our home away from home – the downstairs bar of the Flora Hotel. It seemed that Robbie had been given a reprieve and was to stay with the group a while longer, Ron was willing to accept my solution of staying ostensibly with Antonia and so in the morning we were to leave. Life and joy returned to my disembodied spirit and I became a whole person once more. The cognac–vermouth flowed and I sat close to Ron, safe again in the aura that surrounded us, listening to his voice, watching his movements, the way his brown hands with their long fingers played with the glass, the precise Britishness of his clipped accent, the sleek fine blond hair and the green eyes that only occasionally were allowed to meet mine. The emotions between us were so strong that it was almost tangible. Every now and then I glanced over at Robbie who was drinking as heartily as the rest of us, but punctuating his swallows with a squirming and scratching that reminded me of a mother monkey picking fleas. After watching for a while I noticed him rubbing his arms and I asked what was the matter. "Oh nothing," was the reply.

"Nonsense Robbie," I said, "you look like a bloody monkey sitting there scratching. Roll up your sleeve and let me have a look." Reluctantly he turned back his cuff exposing his forearm and there I recognized the unmistakable pustules of scabies. Having been afflicted myself early in the war I knew what to look for. I burst out laughing. "Hell's bells, Robbie – you've got scabies!" I choked out between giggles.

But Robbie didn't share the joke. He drew himself up haughtily. "Nonsense Mara," he said stiffly. "An officer in His Majesty's Navy doesn't get scabies!"

"Oh Robbie," I said, "have it your own way, but you'd better do something about it, or at least have it seen to if you won't believe me." Needless to say he didn't and a month later ended up back at the naval hospital in Livorno having sulfur baths, as by that time he was covered from head to foot and very uncomfortable.

We made quite a night of it and it was a hungover group that met the next morning for the ride to Florence. A stop at the Flora was not a luxury, it was a necessity and so it was late when we finally got on the road. It was cold and crowded and I was sitting on a box of rations jammed between the two front seats and after a while it started to rain and since the windshield wiper didn't work I worked it by hand so that Ron could see. My arms ached and my backside was numb and I knew I couldn't hold out until Florence. Ordinarily the trip should take about seven hours. We wanted to get over the Radicofani Pass while it was still light as we didn't know if it had yet snowed up there and it was a bad bit of going at the best of times. It was with a sigh of relief that we flew down the last steep grade and leveled off, making for Siena and it was an even greater relief to me when Ron and Robbie decided it would be better to spend the night there.

Siena at that time was a closed city – only military were allowed in and there was a strict curfew. We were stopped at the gates by an M.P. and asked for our travel orders. When I presented my papers the soldier come closer and peered into my face. "If I was a Roosevelt I wouldn't be riding around this country in no jeep," he remarked as he handed them back. Ron and I were convulsed – we both remembered a New Yorker cartoon showing the bottom of a coal mine and one miner turning to another and saying, "My God, it's Eleanor Roosevelt!"

We fumbled our way through the narrow cobble-stoned streets until we found the military hotel and then the process of registering became somewhat embarrassing. Ron signed us in – Commander Ronald Lena, Lt. Wm. Robinson, Marine driver Fred Hale and Mrs. Margaret Roosevelt. The soldier on duty looked at us rather strangely and remarked that there was plenty of accommodation for enlisted men but that the officers would have to share a room. We tried to be nonchalant and said that was perfectly all right, but when we saw the room it contained only one double bed. It was too late for dinner so we had a couple of shots of cognac and all piled in – Ron in the middle, Robbie on one side and I on the other. I have no doubt that Fred got the best night's sleep of any of us. Apparently, there was no mess in the hotel, so the next morning we sent Robbie out to the jeep to see what he could dig up for breakfast. What he returned with was a tin of salmon and some tea bags. To me, tea in the morning is more of an emetic than anything else, but I wanted something hot and I didn't want to start the day on cognac. The salmon tasted pretty awful right out of the can, but I was more worried about putting my face on and not holding up the men with too much primping. As a rule it takes me hours, nor was I going to make any concession to circumstances, so I did the best I could with lipstick and mascara which I always applied with a needle, to everyone's horror. It was sheer hell to put make up on with men looking at you and to feel rushed. Usually I get up two hours ahead of time and sneak into the bathroom to perform this transformation as I refuse to sleep in make up – this made for some pretty long days, but at least I had the satisfaction of knowing that my eye make up was in place and since at that time I had very long lashes it was a kind of security blanket behind which to hide.

It was a lovely day, bright and rain-washed and we pulled out of Siena and in no time were flying down the hill past Poggibonsi, the scene of Robbie's wipeout, and on into Florence. Ron dropped me off at Antonia's house and promised to come back for dinner – and to bring some food.

Then began a nightmarish time, which I only remember in bits and pieces. Antonia had two children, a boy and a girl, and they always seemed to be crawling on my bed in front of the fireplace. Her husband was a prisoner of war in Libya and Antonia kept trying to get news of him through Ron. There was nothing to do except try and keep warm and to wait for Ron to show up. Robbie kept us supplied with wood and news and from what he said the household in via Menotti was showing symptoms of disintegration. Tourneau, the young paratrooper, had left and O'Hara was still doing his devious best to put Ron in bad stead with the authorities and so we both had to be careful. It was a gruesome time, physically uncomfortable and mentally demoralizing. There was no work to keep me busy. The Germans were stalemated up north and Florence was being held by a token force which was gradually giving way to Military Government and civilian rule. Everybody was waiting for reassignment. I don't think we ever went out – I only remember sitting in front of the fireplace and talking to Antonia – and always the same refrain. Ron and myself, myself and Ron, and what was to become of us. The war was over enough for me to start worrying about the future and this turned out to be worse than living in fear. December arrived, cold, grey and windy, but with the happy news that O'Hara had left. I moved back to Ciro Menotti and the next day Celestino – our chef, our cordon bleu – left. Ron, Robbie and Fred were left to my culinary ministrations, which I had to perform on a coal stove for which the only fuel was lignite. Lignite is hard to get burning and sent out continual billows of acrid smoke. My eyes swelled and watered and the food was never really quite cooked, just grey with the smoke and raw on the inside. We ate dinner at the Excelsior mess so I only had to struggle with morning toast and tea. Ron and I were together, but it wasn't a happy time. We knew the sands were running out and since he refused to talk about it I didn't dare.

December 12. Evening. Cocktail time at the Excelsior. Ron and I were sitting in a far corner at a table against the wall. "I have to send you back to Rome again, love," he said. I just sat there. He unfastened his ID bracelet, gold link with blue enamel insignia. "This was given to me when I left," he said. "If anyone notices it's gone I'll say it got caught crawling under a barbed wire. I want you to have it." He put it around my wrist. It was much too big. I sat there with the tears running down my cheeks. There was nothing more to say. Ron ordered another round of drinks.

Robbie and Fred were to drive me down. We left in the grey early morning about ten days before Christmas. The jeep was loaded with gear. Fred drove and Robbie, fortified by a British breakfast of porridge, which I had tried to whip up through the smoke and the swollen eyes, sang lusty naval songs as we drove out of the city. We took the Siena road, which we knew so well, every mile of which held memories. All went well until we reached the outskirts of Poggibonsi and then our luck ran out. We were detouring around a bridge when we found that the road had been closed off. There was a dreary looking peasant standing guard holding a limp red flag and he informed us that the Bailey bridges had been washed out and that we would have to go back and over the mountains to take the Arezzo road. That meant a long climb, and it was cold, bitterly cold. My forehead ached, and my hands and feet were numb and the GI pants I wore seemed made of some porous material. We started back. The road unwound before us in all the austerity and bleakness of the Tuscan landscape with its miniature canyons tortuously eroded into a Raphael background up which swept a snow-laden wind through Browning's "gash in the wind-grieved Apennines." Curve after curve melted behind us when suddenly, rounding a hairpin twist, we came upon a huge lorry parked by the side of the road and three "pongos" placidly brewing tea over a brushwood fire. We pulled up and made for the fire. Soon we were all chatting cozily and I had pulled my shoes off and wrapped my feet in a blanket and the pongos had swapped a bottle of Mistra for some of our cigarettes. I think that Mistra is purely an Italian concoction, although its counterpart may be encountered in Africa where it goes under the name of arack and in France where it is known as absinthe and damned hard to get. About all that can be said for it is that it is alcohol and that's just what I needed on this trip. Lots of alcohol so as not to think. After a few good pulls at the bottle we all felt better. The blood began to circulate once more and as we started off again our Royal Marine Fred sniffed the cold air like a race horse and put the jeep at the hills with more than his usual abandon. He was a bloody good driver.

We had scarcely gone a hundred yards when he pulled up with a jerk that nearly sent me through the windscreen. "Mr. Robinson, sir, may I borrow your revolver, sir?" In a daze Robbie handed over his sidearm and Fred flew over a hedge by the side of the road and raced off into a field. Several shots rang out and Robbie and I found ourselves prone on the floor of the jeep, inching our noses up over the side to see what was going on.

In the middle of the field stood a flock of eleven large white geese. As each shot blasted at them they waddled a few steps in one direction and then in the other, never breaking formation nor hurrying. By this time, Fred had abandoned his attempts to plug one and was running madly in pursuit taking flying leaps at his quarry, only to land on his face in the mud as his prey sidled just beyond his reach. Helpless with laughter we watched as he finally landed on top of a large, tough looking gander. In a moment he was back through the hedge and the struggling, squawking bird was thrust into my arms and we were off just as a farmer materialized from nowhere and rushed after us down the road brandishing a pitch-fork.

The rest of the ride was nightmare. The goose squirmed and dirtied and interfered with the gearshift. Finally, I tied it up in Robbie's raincoat and put it on the floor as a footwarmer where it made strange grunting noises.

We arrived in Rome after being twelve hours on the road and made for the nearest pub, which turned out to be in a British mess. In my GI pants and with a now quiescent goose under one arm I strode up to the bar and ordered six cognac–vermouths. I had planned to leave the animal in the lobby but since, on entering, I had over-heard one officer turn to another and say, "I say, looks like Christmas already, doesn't it?" I thought it wiser to keep it with me.

By the time we had finished the drinks and eaten some corned beef it was late. I couldn't bear the thought of going home, of spending the night alone in my cold dismal villa, so I had Robbie take me to Gemma's home. I had a key and everyone was asleep when I got there. Quietly I let myself in, shut the goose in the bathroom and groped in the sister's room for a vacant bed.

I was still sleeping soundly the next morning when movement in the bedroom seeped through my semi-consciousness. I heard Anna say, "There's a goose in the bathroom!"

Gemma's voice mumbled something indistinct. Then there was a chorus, Nanda and Gabriella, *le sorelline*, "There's a goose in the bathroom!"

Feeling as if somewhere, somehow, I had lived through all this before and mindful of the famous "horse in the bathroom" joke I opened my eyes and said loudly and distinctly, "1 know. I put it there." Then I went back to sleep.

The next day I returned to villa Albani. Ron had promised me Christmas and we went for dinner to Ranieri, my favorite restaurant, near the Piazza di Spagna. We both tried to make it a cheerful meal – Ron had been ordered back to England for reassignment. After dinner we returned to the villa and sat in front of the fireplace. There was nothing left to say so we held hands waiting for the sound of the jeep horn which would mean that Fred had arrived to take Ron to Naples. The next day I wrote in my diary: "Ron has left, a phase of my life is closed and as far as I'm concerned there will be no more life for me until we are together again." I did not believe that such suffering was possible. If I could only have the hope that things will work out for us perhaps it would be of some comfort. As it is I go about in a daze with the tears too near the surface to allow me even to talk over the telephone. Life is a blackout everywhere I turn and I have an actual physical pain that gnaws at me day and night. Every small thing is full of poignant memories too recent to be borne. I didn't think I could love like this, I pray that it is not "too late" as Ron seems to think. At first

I thought that I could not break up a family and build my happiness on someone else's unhappiness, but now I'm not sure. I would do anything to have Ron – anything that he would not regret. I love him so much that all the rest of my life will not be too long to dedicate to him. BUT – "years are the shells of life, and empty shells when they hold only days, and days, and days." Yes, Mr. Edwin Arlington Robinson.

On January 4, I found this unsent letter in my diary:

Ron my beloved,
You have been gone now for ten days and still I have no word. I do not dare to write to you – yet. The very fact of addressing my letter to Canada makes me realize the gulf in space and – perhaps – spirit, that separates us. You have gone on to "fresh woods and pastures new" while I remain behind, always the sadder fate, among scenes and people and sounds that are still fresh with your presence. And while my whole being still cries out in almost physical pain at this separation I still cannot picture your whereabouts, what you are doing, who you are with. My life resolves itself into one long ache to look at you, to hold you, to feel you close to me again. I hear your voice a thousand times a day, the pet names you called me, delicious in their novelty and because it was you who spoke them. I relive our last meeting, and so poignant is the memory that I run to the window expecting to see the jeep outside the cancello and your face peering up at me. Oh Ron, darling, if memories must hurt so perhaps it had been better not to have made them. Not to have spent that last night in your arms by the firelight. Noel Coward would have been proud of us! Have you special things that hurt you to tears as I have? Does the sound of an iron gate slamming shut do to you what the sound of a jeep horn does to me? Above all else in life I cling to the thought of our next meeting. I am afraid of what I shall find. That your scruples will have gotten the better of your love for me and that you will want the bracelet

back. Will you remember the night you gave it me? Had you premeditated your action? Or was it on the spur of the moment because we were both beautifully tight and feeling sentimental? I shall always love Florence because for me it has only one set of memories – and all of them are you. I cannot keep on telling you how much I love you. Words are inadequate and my heart is so full that I fear to shock you with extravagant phrases. If I tell you that you are my life I can but realize that that is the cheapest thing I can offer you. My love, you may not want, or it may only hurt you. I feel myself inadequate to guarantee your future or else I would say with Juliet, "divorce your family and renounce your world and I'll no longer be but your love and your comrade and your slave.

On January 27 came a long-awaited letter from England:

Darling, I am still being kicked around by the powers that be and therefore getting nowhere fast. I keep my thoughts on our next meeting and do so hope that you have been able to make some arrangements to get back to the USA. Here, beloved, I sit in the kitchen for the same reason that you and I sat in your kitchen, it's so bloody cold there is no way of producing heat in any other room in the house. I am in a little town in Surrey a mile and a half from the nearest pub and therefore almost like the Sahara. The Canadian Navy is trying to make up its mind what is to be done with me, therefore I pine for action of some kind, but may get it in the shape of a trip to the Far East.

Beloved, every piece of music I hear reminds me of you and every drink I have I wish I were having it with you. I often feel that all the blame is mine, I should have been a good boy and gone away. But it seems that I wanted it that way and I still want it that way. I can see you best when you used to come to the balcony and wave on my arrival from the north. How I miss you and how I plan and scheme for the future. Do you think of me, and do you too look forward to the day when we shall meet again? Don't, beloved, do something or anything silly. Don't get bored with life, for I am worried and then naturally get prompted by the green-eyed monster. I wonder who you are with and then what you are doing. What a man I am. I always wanted all. But while I am on the subject I might as well tell you how happy I have been and how many thanks (a poor word) I owe you for all.

Now let me tell you about Robbie. He and I traveled from the north together and we had a frightful do in London. We had a lot to drink and then, wanting more we needs must go to a "bottle" club where we polished off two bottles of gin. What a hangover for both of us! The theme all night was "remember Ranieri", "remember the Flora", and so it went on. I miss you at every turn and have only your photos to talk to, but honey, I get no reply. Oh me!

And so, for a few short days, goodbye. Please be careful so that we meet again soon, I don't like this life unless I can be close to you. Much of all my love you have now, beloved, all I can add is my hope for the future. I believe in it.

Soon I became ill. The cold, the damp, the tears, the lack of food. Poor dear Ada, so loyal, so affectionate, did her best. Out in the early cold to stand in line, hauling water from the street fountains, why did it never enter my mind to help her? I went to bed and hoped for another pneumonia, which I was determined not to cure, but Gemma found out. She sent an ambulance for me and once again I was in their home with all the sisters. After a while I started going out again, but it was no fun – I remember coming back one night after dinner with an Allied officer laden with cigarettes and Hershey bars. I was a bit tight and very angry and I threw everything on the bedroom floor and stamped and stamped screaming, "They treat me like an Italian whore – I don't want their damn chocolate!" And so it went.

Finally, I got word that a friend of my father, Myron Taylor, had been named representative to the Vatican and it was suggested that he might be influential in getting me passage home. I called, and he invited me for tea. We had a nice visit and he promised he would do what he could. I walked home in the dark with tears running down my face. There was a full moon.

Several weeks later I was put on a plane for Naples together with Giuli to await transport. I remember that Margaret Bourke-White, the famous photographer, was on the same flight.

We went to a hotel and waited. Eventually we boarded a troop transport and went across to Oran to pick up a convoy. The ship I was on was repatriating a group of fliers who had fought at the Kasserine Pass. Years later, when I saw the movie *Paton* with its intense opening scene, the fading trumpets in the background, I thought of those boys. Every evening there was machine-gun practice on deck, which was fun. Poor little Giuli was seasick and it took us three weeks to reach New York.

My father met me at the ship and we went to his apartment and I met his new wife. It was not a happy meeting. The next afternoon I was sitting in the living room when the butler came in with a bottle of gin on a silver tray – God – Robbie! I was back in the villa in Florence – Robbie was saying, "One day you will be sitting in your father's home on Park Avenue and the butler will come in with a bottle of gin on a silver tray and you will know that Robbie has arrived!"

Truly it was he. How glad I was, how I hugged and embraced him. He was passing through on his way to, I forget where, but I joyed in his presence for the short time that we could be together.

Most of what followed was meaningless. I weathered the summer in a little cottage on my father's estate in Oyster Bay, but the anxiety attacks and the nightmares grew worse. Autumn came and I lasted just long enough to see Giuli set out for school in her little Chapin uniform – light green tunic and white blouse, and then I signed myself into the Payne Whitney Psychiatric Pavillion of the New York Hospital. I did not know if psychiatric treatment could do anything for me, but it was a refuge. The memories continued:

> Always a blank wall. The wall and the white feeling in the pit of the stomach. Hanging on – marking time by quarter hours. So much time gone and I am still alive. The tightness comes up and up, distorting vision, slowing down the reactions, emphasizing the clarity of sound, each item a disintegrated quality. Waiting. Poised in the predatory grip of a vacuum surrounded by dangers. Fear is without eyes. It is grey, always whisking around corners. Sometimes it is behind and I am afraid to turn; sometimes it is ahead and I am afraid to advance. It peers and shuffles and refuses to announce itself, coy of being recognized. I feel the tension mounting. Unbearably wave after wave starts at the tips of my toes and sweeps upward until it reaches my lungs, my heart. The feeling of being stifled forces me to my feet, out of bed if it is night, into the hall if it is daylight. What brings it on? Waiting? Waiting for something to happen; someone to come; the ring of a doorbell, the thud of a letter in the box, each sense alert for a familiar step, a voice, a faintly remembered smell. A blind frustration of disappointment turns in upon myself and causes a gnawing hunger that has nothing to do with appetite.

Mrs. Tupper joined our group one prematurely hot day in April. She was admitted onto the fifth floor, which was removed from the fourth and graduating floor by only one elevator stop in space, but by month upon dreary month of treatment and therapy and boredom and anticipation in time. We were a dull group. Some of us had worked our way down from the uninhibited regions of seven by virtue of prolonged baths and shock treatment. We had reached the threshold of normalcy and were being poked and prodded across the sill. We didn't like what we saw on the other side, but they wouldn't let us go back.

When Mrs. Tupper entered our lives we were having lunch. She was escorted to the dining room by a nurse and introduced brightly all around by one of the students. It was a way they had of making us feel we were all just guests at an exclusive summer resort. We didn't like it. We didn't like student nurses either. They had a way of eating up anything that was left in the lounge. They would come rustling down the corridor in their starched blue uniforms and exclaim lovingly over a box of candy, "Oh well, just one more piece then if I may, Mrs. Kelly." They were always very careful to remember our names correctly – and the first thing you knew the whole thing was gone. They were always hungry. Poor things, we gave them a rough time. We couldn't get away with anything with the floor nurse so we took it out on them. It wasn't malicious. Just a kind of game. There was one, though, whom we hated. Miss Brindler. She walked like a graduate already, duck-footed, and took a smug pleasure in trying to push us around. She had a big smug face too, as bland and uninteresting as cold lamb fat. We got even with her. One afternoon someone smuggled in a box of matches and we set fire to the curtains in the sun parlor while she was on duty. It was just a small fire but it took some of the starch out of her. Well, at any rate, the students lasted only six weeks and then moved on to some other department of the hospital and we would have a whole new batch to break in to our eccentricities. Mrs. Tupper was a large, melancholy woman with an infuriating air about her. She had bright orange hair and big gray eyes with big black circles under them. She sat down at my table and started to mess her food about on her plate. I didn't like that and made a mental note to ask to be moved. Food was the only thing I wanted in life and I had no patience with people who would only play around with it. If they couldn't eat it, let them give it to me. I very often got two or three meals at a time this way, when the nurses weren't looking, of course. I had a standing arrangement with one of the other patients whom I had bullied into slipping me her second cup of coffee. Mrs. Tupper saw me glaring at her.

"Nice lunch, isn't it?" she murmured. I didn't answer. "Lovely place, too," she added. I was watching to see if she was going to eat her dessert. She leaned toward me. "Only you wouldn't think they'd allow all those cats to be wandering around in the corridors." I looked at her and forgot momentarily about the dessert. If she was batting this far out of our league, this was going to be fun. Next morning I controlled my appetite long enough to ask her how she had slept. "Oh, just fine," she said brightly, although the circles looked to me bigger and blacker than the day before. "Except, of course, for the cats," she added.

"What about them?" I asked.

"Oh, they were on and off the bed all night," she replied. I departed for the garden hoping that the doctors wouldn't catch on and send her up to six, or maybe even seven, before I could get back.

★

I came back from the garden. The heat was stifling. It was going to be a bad day for me. The heat – that was it. I leaned against the casement of the window that would open out only just so far. I tried to concentrate on the building across the way, and the East River shining in the early sun. But it was no use. Sounds grew sharper and brighter. The light changed; the building got farther away; a strange, sweet smell of burning:

The alleyway is deserted. From the kitchen window I look through the house next door and see a bidet dangling obscenely from a third-story landing. The silence creeps over the rubble and rises up in little puffs of dust and settles again like fog. The planes have just passed over; we can expect them back. At the end of the alley stands the garage. A point of flame flicks out from underneath the door. Flicks out and withdraws like the tongue of a snake. Slowly the door opens and a man comes out. Slowly, slowly he starts up the alley. He is aflame from foot to head. In the stillness I can hear the faint sizzle as he nears my window. His feet are shape-less red lumps. His shirt has been burned off and his bare arms and back rise in juicy welts that are not blisters, but the crisped fat of roasting meat. The flames shoot from his hair and fall back down onto his face. He walks steadily, step after step, and as he passes near me I see his eyes turned for a moment toward mine. They are

161

bright with agony, but unseeing. Enveloped in flame he passes noiselessly into the street where he falls down without a cry. The fire burns stronger now, and a strange odor mingles with the acrid air that hangs over the debris.

★

Mrs. Tupper was moved up to seven. For a few days I wasn't well enough myself to get up to the library, our communal news exchange point, where for a brief half hour the various floors mingled and gossiped under the watchful and prying eyes of the nurses and librarians. Vague and wonderful reports sifted down of her antics. How one night she swung from the window drapes emitting Tarzan-like yells, and from there jumped to the chandelier which crashed all over the floor in glorious confusion. After that came a spell where she claimed her throat was paralyzed and spent her time in bed scribbling naughty words to the doctors on a piece of scratch paper. By the end of six weeks she was back with us again, subdued, eager to please as ever, her big gray eyes mutely apologetic. The horde of cats had been reduced to one old Tom, which she called Bozo. Gradually, the whole floor became attached to him, and he became as much a part of our daily life as the hurry-up-and-wait system by which we were shepherded from one activity to another. Occupational therapy was my particular cross. Mrs. Tupper would sit before her loom and weave with the frenzy of the true artist watching the patterns blend themselves and take form into the dozens of place mats, centerpieces and doilies which she turned out as if following some inner, secret ritual. I was no hand at crafts. I set up an easel in a corner of the studio between two windows where I could dream my own dreams in peace and daub my vague shadows on the canvas without interference. Slowly a mountain took shape, and a road. Always the same road...

Why do we always seem to hit the Radicofani as it grows dark? The shadows are creeping up the gullies and the cold stillness hangs in the air with the poised sun, crouching and bitter. The lonely road stretches ahead, lost behind us, losing itself before us, each crest drawing us on with the promise of the plain below. The desolate Umbrian landscape, scarred by nature, takes to itself the further scars of war. Here they form and integrate. The overturned German tanks still flaunting their grim swastikas dominate the other flotsam of abandoned material. Fawn colored road flanked by reddish precipices hemmed in by grey-purple mountains, beautiful, bleak monotony.

On the summit of the pass there is a level stretch. To the right a sizable hillock mounts, blotting out the view of one of the distant mountain villages, which silhouettes its rows of cypresses like a dinosaur vertebrae. I watch for the cross that tops it. On one of our trips we came unexpectedly upon a stray army truck of sepoys. It was pulled up alongside the road under the lee of a Wehrmacht tank, its midget occupants engaged in digging a grave. Now, only the lonely cross stands, dramatic and a bit wistful in the evening mists that early wind up through the ravines. A fine burial place – unencumbered. A tin helmet perched on the cross slats against it in the stronger gusts...

★

It was three in the morning. Everyone else was asleep. Mrs. Tupper and I sat in the lounge smoking cigarettes. It was an idle hour – the night nurse sat in her cubbyhole at the end of the corridor where a dim light burned. Fog was on the river and the light of the street was haloed. Mrs. Tupper was cradling Bozo in her arms. I saw the river, and I saw the street and it was as if I was seeing them for the first time.

Spring came. On April 10, I received the following signal. "Arriving Boston 21 or 22 HMS *Antigua*, much love, Ron." I signed myself out and took the train for Boston. I engaged a room at the Copley Plaza, ordered champagne and *hors d'oeuvres* and took a tender to *Antigua* anchored in the harbor. Ron was waiting for me in the wardroom and we went ashore. Back in the hotel room we opened the bottle and were about to toast our reunion when the phone rang, it was the front desk. "Are you entertaining a gentleman in your room?"

"Of course," I said. "Why do you think I ordered the wine and all those *hors d'oeuvres*?"

"We do not permit that," the person said. I was speechless. *Boston*! We checked out and went to some commercial hotel, the kind where you have to wrestle the bed down out of the wall. The next day we took the train back to New York and Ron accompanied me to the hospital and up to my room. We sat together on the hospital bed. "Is there nothing, nothing – no way out?" I asked desperately.

"No, poppet. This is the end. We both know it. Do you remember what you said last night? It was prophetic. You said 'the sands are running out' and you quoted 'Tristram' again, something about 'the wearing out of life on a racked length of days'. You were right. They have run out sooner than we thought."

"I can't bear it. There must be some way to alleviate the pain. Some compromise. I'll blow my top."

Ron stiffened. "No you won't. There's so much more in you than you know. Some day you'll realize it. You're beautiful. You're young. You have a whole life ahead of you."

"Yes. A whole life of minutes and days and years that have to be filled."

"Perhaps I'm luckier. I have a job of work to do. I shall go back and play a part and nobody will ever know. But how should I feel if you did something foolish and some day someone should say to me, 'You used to know Mara, didn't you? Look what's happened to her'."

"No, no darling. I didn't mean that. I just meant – well, you know how it is. I'm just no good when you're not around. You remember, even in Italy. People – if you're there I enjoy them. I enjoy myself. It's different with you. You can have fun wherever you are, whomever you're with."

"I'm a bloody good actor if that's what you mean. I can make people feel that I'm a good sort of chap, whereas you're always bored. You always were. Or perhaps you're franker than I am. You don't care enough about people to put on an act."

"That's only true when you're not around, darling. Remember what fun we used to have together? I liked everybody then."

"You and I have always been lone wolves, pet. Why do I always have to preach when I'm around you? You've met so many attractive chaps worth so much more than I am. You had to fall for me. Well, I should have pulled out, but I didn't. I wanted to have my cake and eat it too.

Now we're both paying." His shoulders shook and he got up and walked to the bureau. "Thank God for Kleenex, the great American invention. Look pet, I'm going."

"No, please, I'll be good. It's only a quarter after nine. You can stay until ten o'clock. We'll talk about something else."

"Twisting the knife."

"What will you do when you leave here? Where will you go?"

"To Tony's. To get roaring drunk. Only I know that I can't get drunk."

"Oh good. Can't I come too? Just for tonight?"

"If you were coming too there wouldn't be any need to get roaring drunk."

We looked at each other and I choked and the tears started – "Poppet... We did better in Italy, didn't we darling? Strong army type breaks down. If it's raining when you leave here it will be quite Hemingway, won't it?"

"You know, sometimes in here I wish that I could draw. I see things so vividly and I want to put them down. You remember the time we were driving in the jeep over a mountain pass and it was toward sunset and we were hurrying so as to make Florence before curfew? All of a sudden we rounded a curve and there was part of an Indian convoy drawn up by the side of the road. Three sepoys were standing on top of a small hill digging a grave. I can see the cross silhouetted against the evening sky, and the dim mountains in the distance. I want to paint that lonely cross."

"So many things to remember."

"Ron – why does it have to be this way?"

"We've been into all that."

"I know. I'm sorry."

Again we looked at each other photographing each feature. "Will you promise me something? That from now on you'll look ahead. There are beautiful years ahead. That you'll stay here and get cured. These people can help you."

"Will we write to each other?"

"I've thought about that."

"Yes, I've thought about it too."

"You see. We've both thought about it because we know it's something we shouldn't do. Every letter would only be the reopening of an old wound. Each time we sat down – no, darling, we shan't write."

"Promise me only one thing then, that if ever…"

"Yes. If ever my life does blow up, I'll let you know."

"Any place. Any time. Five, ten years from now I'll be there."

"You mustn't count on it, though. You mustn't think about it."

"I won't."

"You see, angel, you and I have lived our finest part of life. Six months of living in an entire lifetime doesn't seem much, but we have something that no one can ever take away from us. You *are* my life."

"And you will always be mine, Ron."

We both rose and with tears streaming down both our faces, we clasped each other for a last time.

"I'll walk you to the elevator, darling," I said. "You have to be unlocked out of here you know." Hand in hand we went down the corridor towards the nurse in charge. In silence we waited for the lift. Ron stepped inside, turning his face to the wall to fumble for the buttons.

"Cheer-ho, beloved. *Arrivederci*, as we say in Italy."

The door slammed shut and I walked back to my room.

Aftermath

Giuli made a lovely marriage. Her young husband was doing his military service in the Marines and they were stationed in Florida on maneuvers. One day I received a strange letter from her:

"Dearest Mina," she wrote (short for mammina, her pet name for me). "I don't know what could have happened to me, but all of a sudden I heard machine gun fire and then I found myself wandering in a strange part of town cradling my kitten in my arms. After a long time Randy found me." I thought – Flashback.

Four months later she was dead – killed in a plane crash on her way home from a visit to her father in Italy. In less than a month she would have celebrated her twenty-second birthday.

Epilogue

This little book has been incubating for over fifty years. Numerous starts were made and discontinued. I tried writing it in the third person. Glossing over events, disguising characters to make them more heroic, but they only came out unreal and phony. Finally, it dawned on me what I suppose should have been obvious all along. Tell the story as it happened. Most of the principal characters are dead and since it no longer matters to me to cut a heroic figure, that is what I have done. All of the first part is taken from a diary I kept at the time and from notes I made immediately after arriving in this country in 1945. The rest I have lived with constantly for all these years and so was easy to reconstruct from letters and memories. Whether it will be of interest to anyone other than myself seemed of little consequence while it was being written – now, however, I feel that perhaps there is some merit in one story of war told from a strictly female, civilian point of view. I dedicate these memories to the men and women of 5th Army in Italy who saved and changed my life for ever.

Years ago I read an interview with Audie Murphy – World War II's most decorated soldier – in which he was asked, "How do people survive a war?"

He thought for a moment, then replied, "I don't think they ever do."

In Another Country tells the dramatic story of one woman's experience of war and love. Her passion for Italy, coupled with a desire to escape family pressures, drew Margaret Roosevelt into an abusive, constrictive marriage to an Italian, and a precarious situation in the war-torn Italy of the 1930s. Wanted by the S.S. and forced into hiding with a young child during the war, Margaret was to go to work for an Allied Intelligence group after the liberation, and embark on a passionate, tangled affair that would awaken previously unknown feelings of love, of belonging, of loss and of desolation.

Margaret Roosevelt's vividly drawn, engaging recollections share the most intimate of feelings and provide a precious glimpse of a time, for many, assigned to the history books, but which should never be forgotten.

Crayon drawing of author by Michel Werboff, 1966 — Russian portrait painter who is represented in the Prado, Madrid and the Metropolitan Museum of Art, New York.

US $16.95

ISBN 1-930493-06-1

9 781930 493063

margaret roosevelt

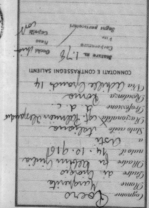

IN ANOTHER COUNTRY